Love
and
Power
in the
Stepfamily

Love
and
Power
in the
Stepfamily

JAMIE KELEM KESHET

McGRAW-HILL BOOK COMPANY
New York   St. Louis   San Francisco
Hamburg   Mexico   Toronto

To Harry and David

1 2 3 4 5 6 7 8 9 DOCDOC 8 7 6

ISBN 0-07-034246-6

LIBRARY OF CONGRESS CATALOGING-IN-PUBLICATION DATA

Keshet, Jamie Kelem.
Love and power in the stepfamily.
Bibliography: p.
Includes index.
1. Stepfamilies—United States.   2. Stepparents—United States.
3. Stepchildren—United States.
I. Title.
HQ759.92.K47 1987   306.8'74   86-10471
ISBN 0-07-034246-6

BOOK DESIGN BY BETH TONDREAU

Contents

Acknowledgments

When I started planning this book I was the mother of an infant and a preschooler. I bought a portable electric typewriter to use at home on the first draft. Now, as the book is nearing publication, I have two sons in elementary school and I do my writing on a word processor.

Many people have helped me in this endeavor. David Kantor taught me to think about families as systems, to trust my mind, and to develop my ideas more clearly. Irene Pierce Stiver offered support and encouragement through the many stages of writing and rewriting.

I am particularly indebted to the wonderful people who have cared for my children and freed my mind for work. Patricia Williams has excelled both as a child-care provider and office manager. The teachers of the Russell Cooperative Preschool and the Newton Toddler Program have given loving care to my sons.

Swamis Muktananda and Chidvilasananda of the Siddha lineage have taught me the importance of welcoming each other with love and respect. I hope some of their love is captured in the book.

My own family has played an important role. My husband, Harry, has given me support at every level. He has encouraged me, reviewed my ideas, listened to my anxieties, cared for our children, and taken me away from it all. His faith has kept me going. My stepson Matt has enriched my understanding of stepparenting, and my sons Ezra and Daniel have educated me as a parent.

Finally, I wish to thank the many stepparents and remarried parents who have participated in my groups, come to my lectures, and worked with me in counseling. My understanding of the stepfamily has grown in response to their problems and dilemmas. Their stories are the raw material I have used to share my knowledge. I hope that other families will benefit from my interpretations of their experiences.

CHAPTER ONE
Getting Acquainted

*T*hink back to the birth of your first child or, if you are not a parent yourself, the birth of a friend's child. The new parents are congratulated by friends and family. Gifts and greetings pour in for weeks. People come to visit the new arrival. Advice is offered. The new parents know that they can ask for help and find out what is ahead from more experienced parents all around them.

Now think about the day you became a stepparent. Perhaps you cannot even pinpoint a day on which you moved from the ambiguous role of Dad's (or Mom's) friend to that other ambiguous role of stepparent. Perhaps what comes to mind is your wedding day. You may have received good wishes, gifts, and advice on your marriage, but did anyone congratulate you for becoming a stepmother? Did anyone offer advice on how to be a good stepfather? Did anyone ask you how it felt to move into this new and vague role?

If you are like most stepparents, your friends and relatives probably glossed over the fact that you were getting a package deal in your marriage. And if anyone did ask, you may have been too embarrassed to express your real feelings. How could you admit that you, an adult, were sometimes jealous of those stepchildren-to-be and were not at all sure you wanted them living in your home? Least of all could you share these doubtful feelings with your new partner, who was so sensitive about your acceptance of the children.

Since that eventful day how many greeting cards have been sent to you as stepmom or stepdad on your birthday or on Mother's or Father's Day? How many teachers have invited you to join in your stepchild's school parties, plays, and conferences? How many of your friends have understood when you tried to share the confusion and turmoil of your new role?

What if you are the remarried parent? Who has given you support for the difficult job of holding it all together? Did anyone give you Super Glue as a wedding present? When your friends tell you how lucky you are that your new wife is so sweet to your children, do you dare tell them about the Sunday nights after the weekend visits, the hurt feelings, the missed messages? Has anyone told you the secret of cutting yourself into enough pieces to satisfy your new partner, your children, your parents, your boss, and your former partner? I doubt it.

Whether you are a stepparent in Omaha, Nebraska, who has never talked to anyone about how it feels to be a stepparent or a remarried parent in Newark, New Jersey, who is convinced that every other remarried parent has already solved the dilemmas you face, you will be reassured to know that you are not alone. In the 1980s an estimated 1.5 million second marriages are taking place each year.[1] Of these marriages, 60 percent include a parent who has custody of a child under the age of eighteen, and 20 percent involve a parent without custody.[2] That comes to about 1,200,000 new stepfamilies each year. About one in every five married-couple households includes a partner who has previously been divorced.[3]

If you have recently joined the ranks of the remarried, let me welcome you to stepfamilyhood and offer my congratulations. I have been a stepparent for the last eleven years, a parent for the last eight. Luckily for me, I have had a stepson who does accept me, a husband who listens to me when I have a problem, and training as a teacher and psychotherapist to help me be a better stepparent. In my work as counselor of stepfamilies, I have seen many people who lack the kinds of support I have had. I have heard many sad and complicated stories.

Not that stepparenting is all tears and heartache. It can also be joyous, creative, and exciting. Your stepfamily can surprise you in some wonderful ways. It's not the good times, though, that send you to the library or the bookstore in search of insight.

Many stepparents and remarried parents discover that their previous experience is not enough to guide them through the maze of stepfamily life. The divorce rate for second marriages (55 percent) is higher than the rate for first marriages (50 percent),[4] and the average number of years prior to divorce is lower in second marriages.[5]

Remarried couples need more than love for each other to make marriage a success.

This book provides some specific strategies for making your stepfamily work. Because each family is different, you will have to fill in the details, but I have outlined procedures for solving problems and for talking with your partner. When your family seems to be falling apart at the seams, it is tempting to blame others, to feel like a victim and give up. *But* you don't have to take it lying down. You can make a difference by observing what is happening, setting goals, planning a strategy for change, and acting. You would not give up on a business project that is beginning to falter. You would not drop out of church because your child wasn't picked to star in the Christmas play. I hope you won't give up on your stepfamily either.

STAGES OF THE STEPFAMILY

Understanding your stepfamily can help you to shape it in a way that meets your needs and the needs of other family members. Those of you just entering a stepfamily, or thinking of entering one, may be surprised to hear that stepfamily life can get better after the first few years. The stepfamily's growth follows three stages: acceptance, authority, and affection. Authority is usually the hardest stage, and affection is usually the happiest.

DIFFERENT PERSPECTIVES

When two people remarry and one or both have children, they bring with them very different points of view. If you are a remarried parent, you have undoubtedly felt that your new spouse is insensitive to your children and has outrageous expectations for them. If you are a stepparent, you have probably felt left out and wondered how your partner could tolerate the disrespectful behavior of his or her children.

These differences are natural. Your separate histories and loyalties are not erased when you take marriage vows or move into the same house. In this book I try to bring differences out into the open instead of sweeping them under the rug. Some sections are written from the vantage point of a stepparent, some from the remarried parent's viewpoint. When you read the sections that do not represent your point of view, you may gain some understanding of your partner.

I use the term "marriage" rather loosely. If you and your partner are not married but live together and have a strong commitment to each other, your situation is not very different from that of your neighbors who are married. Most issues result from relationships, not from legal status. If you are considering remarriage, or moving in with someone who is divorced, you can use this book to get a glimpse of what the future may hold.

I also write as though in all divorces both parents share to some degree in raising the children. I do this because I think this is the best situation for most children and also a very difficult one for the parents. If you and your former spouse are both trying to remain involved in your children's lives, you probably need lots of support. If you are in a stepfamily where one of the biological parents has either died or dropped out of the children's lives, you may find some differences from the families I have described. You will also find many similarities.

THE PAIN OF STEPPARENTING

Stepfamilies are different from nuclear families, and this difference may be painful to you. First, there is the pain of feeling left out, not considered, not cared for, by other members of your family. Then there is the pain of having more to give than others will accept from you. This is especially so for stepparents who want to be close to their stepchildren. Finally, there is the pain of living in a family that does not fulfill your ideal of the happy, harmonious, homogeneous nuclear family. This pain is often accompanied by self-blame for the difference.

The material in the book has been presented as lectures to stepfamilies at Riverside Family Institute and at other settings in the Boston area. I tell groups of stepparents and remarried parents the stepfamily facts of life—for example, how all stepchildren chew with their mouths open, or how stepmothers and stepchildren often have their first confrontation over who will sit in the front seat of the car next to Dad. As I talk, couples exchange meaningful glances. There is the laughter of recognition. There is also the relaxation that comes from letting go of individual blame. "So it's not just me," people say afterward.

Even the family of the President of the United States, often referred to as the First Family of the land, has had its difficulties with stepfamily relations, as this story from the *Boston Globe*, December 28, 1984, illustrates:

REAGAN REPORTEDLY TO MEET WITH SON

United Press International

LOS ANGELES—President Ronald Reagan has scheduled peace talks with his eldest son, Michael, to smooth over relations damaged last month in a public squabble between Mrs. Reagan and the younger Reagan, a source close to the Reagan family said yesterday.

The President will also meet his youngest granddaughter, 20-month-old Ashley, for the first time at the meeting today at the Century Plaza Hotel, the source said.

Michael Reagan, his wife, Colleen, and their two children will join the President and Mrs. Reagan for the first time since friction erupted when Mrs. Reagan told a columnist that Michael and his father have become "estranged" over the last three years.

Michael replied on a radio talk show that tension between him and Mrs. Reagan was caused by "jealousy" because he was adopted during Reagan's first marriage to actress Jane Wyman.

Michael, 39, declined to comment on whether he will meet with the President, who arrived in California yesterday for a weeklong New Year's visit. "I made promises to certain people and I'm going to live up to my promise," he said in a telephone interview from his Los Angeles home.

Last month, Michael said he wanted to sit down with his father to settle their differences "outside the press . . . so Dad can get on with negotiating with the Russians."

The source close to the Reagan family said the family has declined to discuss the meeting at the President's request.

LOOKING AT FAMILIES

Imagine watching a baseball game with no prior knowledge of baseball. You observe that some people move quite a bit while others remain in fixed places. After a while, when you have become used to these roles, you see the fixed players leave and others take their places. You think that the man in the center of the diamond-shaped area must be overworked. He is involved with every play, constantly looking about the field, definitely carrying more than his share of the load. You do not know that he is receiving signals from the man who is squatting, that he is excused if he doesn't make many hits, and that he rests for more games than he plays. Focusing on the pitcher results in some misconceptions about the nature of a baseball team.

Observing families can be like watching a baseball game without knowing the rules. We think certain people are in fixed positions and then, seemingly without reason, they rearrange themselves. We are often unaware of the power of the people who are not visibly in the center of the action. If we focus on one person, we often miss the interaction and the nonverbal communication occurring between family members.

In order to view the family more clearly, I use what is called a family systems approach. In family systems, we look at the family as an organization with certain goals, rules, and rituals. Family members do not lose their individuality when we look at them as part of a system. We see them as people with certain important roles in the family as well as personal preferences and styles.

Seeing the family as a system makes it harder to blame individuals for situations that arise. For example, suppose a couple is having a hard time making vacation plans. Finally, one Sunday morning the wife sits her husband down and forces him to choose the motels that he considers suitable. When she gets around to calling the motels, on Thursday afternoon, there are no vacancies. Her husband criticizes her for having waited until Thursday instead of calling on Sunday afternoon. She blames him for not discussing it with her until Sunday or for not calling himself.

In looking at this couple as a system, we wonder whether they share a pattern of not getting it together to enjoy themselves. What unspoken agreement keeps them from doing things right? We see them colluding in not completing the vacation plans on time. Their argument about who is at fault in this particular situation becomes irrelevant.

As I share this way of looking at families with you, I will be using a few terms that I would like to define here:

Boundaries: These are the invisible lines and walls that separate a family from the rest of the community. Within the family, boundaries separate single members or groups of members from each other. Boundaries in a family can be rigid or flexible, open to new people or relatively closed.

Power: Within a family, power is the ability to get something done the way you want it done. Families distribute power in different ways. Usually the adults have greater power and are in a position of authority over the children. Sometimes the power is more evenly divided among children and adults. In some families, one or two members have the greatest share of power.

Stepfamily: A stepfamily consists of two remarried (or living-together) adults, the children of each from former marriages, and any children they have had together in the present marriage. Children who have a primary residence elsewhere and visit them are also considered stepchildren. Couples who have children visiting them, and no children living with them, are considered stepfamily couples.

Stepparent: This is a person who is married to someone who has children. Those children are his or her stepchildren.

New Person: This is an individual who is dating, or in a relationship with, someone who has children from a former marriage.[6] He or she has not married the children's parent or made a permanent commitment to living with him or her and is *not yet* a stepparent. A New Person may or may not go on to become a stepparent.

MINIFAMILIES

When we look at the stepfamily as a family system, we discover that it is made up both of individuals and of groups of people called minifamilies. The *minifamily* is a family unit smaller than a nuclear family—because all its places (i.e., adult male, adult female, and children) are not filled—that nonetheless does the work of a family. A mother and six children, though a family with many members, are called a minifamily because the slot of father or stepfather is vacant. When I use the term "parent-child minifamily," I mean one parent and his or her children. Visiting parents and children form visiting parent-child minifamilies (sometimes shortened to visiting minifamilies); custodial parents and children form custodial parent-child minifamilies (sometimes shortened to custodial minifamilies).

Because minifamilies do have open slots, they can be combined to form stepfamilies. For example, a mother who has custody of one child marries a man with two children. They combine to form a stepfamily. Their stepfamily has the following minifamilies: the new couple, the mother and child, the father and children. The minifamilies do not merge completely into a new nuclear family; within the stepfamily each retains parts of its former identity.

The formerly married couple is also a minifamily. Although a divorce ends the legal marriage, it does not end the emotional relationship the couple has had or the necessity for the couple to communicate about their children. The existence of the exspouse and of the former spouse minifamily is one unique aspect of the stepfamily.

An example will illustrate the usefulness of recognizing the mini-families in stepfamilies. June and Tom, both divorced parents, have been married for six months. June's two sons live with them and visit their father every other weekend. Tom's daughter, Jennifer, visits three weekends out of four. When they are all together, their stepfamily consists of a father-stepfather (Tom), a mother-step-mother (June), and three children (Jennifer, Rick, and Joseph). There are also five minifamilies—June and Tom, June and her children, Tom and his child, June and her ex-husband, Tom and his ex-wife.

June and her sons prepare a surprise birthday party on the Friday night before Jennifer's birthday, which is on Sunday. They plan the party for that night because the boys will be leaving Saturday morning to visit their dad. When Tom and Jennifer come home to a dark house, Rich and Joseph turn on the lights and yell, "Surprise!" There's a big sign on the wall, balloons and flowers decorate the room, and a cake and some presents are arranged on the table.

Jennifer bursts into tears. "But it's not my real birthday," she cries. She buries her head in her hands. Tom, feeling very embarrassed, does not know how to reach out to his daughter or to his new wife and stepsons. June feels hurt. Rick and Joseph look stunned. The rest of the evening is tense and forced. No one quite understands what has happened.

It is tempting at a time like this (and if you are in a stepfamily, you have probably experienced a time like this) to find fault with each other. June might say that Jennifer is spoiled. She might interpret Jennifer's remark ("But it's not my real birthday.") to mean that a child's birthday can only be celebrated with her "real" mother. Tom might say June and her sons have not given Jennifer a chance to make a transition before springing a party on her.

What can we learn about this spoiled birthday party by looking at the minifamilies? Jennifer's mother and father always made a point of celebrating exactly on the day of her birth, even when this meant parties on school days, missing school to go to Grandma's, or staying up late to party after her parents came home from work. Tom and his ex-wife have cooperated to maintain this custom, always allowing Jennifer to spend some part of her birthday with each of them.

June, Rick, and Joseph do not know of this custom in Tom's family. In their minifamily, a birthday celebration is an important act of caring for each other. Their message to Jennifer in planning the surprise is, "We want you to be one of us. We are welcoming you into our family." Planning the surprise may also be a way for their minifamily to feel close to each other. Keeping the secret binds them together, as they were for the two years between June's divorce and her meeting Tom. A surprise party is a way of connecting with Tom and Jennifer *and* of keeping an identity that is separate from them.

Tom and Jennifer, in planning to celebrate on Sunday, Jennifer's real birthday, are not considering the fact that this will mean excluding Rick and Joseph from the party. Keeping their family tradition also keeps them separate from the other minifamily.

Thus, the strong ties of each parent-child minifamily contribute to this unsuccessful birthday party. The one minifamily that could have prevented this confusing event, the couple, is not yet as strong as either parent-child minifamily. June and Tom have not discussed plans for Jennifer's birthday with each other.

An unsuccessful birthday surprise may seem like a small matter in the discussion of such weighty topics as divorce and remarriage. On the contrary, the handling of these special occasions in the second marriage can make a big difference in the family members' feelings about how successful the stepfamily is. As our example shows, carrying off happy celebrations in the stepfamily depends not only on the individuals in the family but on the flexibility of the minifamilies and the communication and cooperation among them.

THE DIVORCED-REMARRIED FAMILY

I have found time and again that the whole system of two divorced parents, their children, and their new spouses often functions as one great big family—somewhat like an extended family. I call this assortment of people and minifamilies the divorced-remarried family. Accepting this as a family is tough for many people, something like accepting the in-laws you are least fond of. A stepfamily that has children from two former marriages becomes part of two different divorced-remarried families. This is one complexity of stepfamily life that we will examine in some detail.

STEPFAMILY DEVELOPMENT

This book follows the development of the stepfamily from the time of your divorce (or your partner's) through the first few years of stepfamily life. In order to understand the stepfamily, we must start with the divorce that preceded it. The formerly married couple become one of the minifamilies of the stepfamily. This changing relationship and its implications for the stepfamily are the subject of Chapter Two. In Chapter Three, we take a close look at the other key minifamily that will form part of the stepfamily, the parent-child minifamily. We will look at both the custodial minifamily and the visiting minifamily and examine their roles in forming the stepfamily.

In Chapter Four we look at the decisive moment when a new relationship has begun and the parent tries to bring together the new-couple minifamily and the parent-child minifamily. This difficult period, when you are not quite a stepfamily, is a time when knowing what is likely to happen and how people are likely to react to one another can be especially helpful.

The three stages of the stepfamily development are described in Chapters Five, Six, and Seven. Chapter Five focuses on the first stage, acceptance, when the family members are learning to think of each other as members of their stepfamily. The family of June and Tom, in our example, was in this stage. In the acceptance stage the minifamilies are torn between joining each other and keeping the ways of living together each has created as a minifamily.

Chapter Six describes the difficult process of authority, establishing the authority of the new-couple relationship over the children. This is the stage at which power is a key issue. The children often feel as though respecting the power and authority of the stepparent is a step down from the power they have gained in the parent-child minifamily. Authority also refers to the power of the new-couple minifamily. The new couple must become the most powerful minifamily, the executive system of the family, in order for their stepfamily to succeed. For many families in counseling, authority seems to be the make-it-or-break-it stage.

In Chapter Seven, we learn about the stage of affection. The mutual acceptance of the stepfamily members in stage one and the resolution of the power issues in stage two pave the way for feelings of warmth, fondness, and attachment to emerge. Because the love felt between steprelations differs from the love between biological relatives, I prefer to call it affection.

The remarried couple are the key to the stepfamily. It is responsible for having brought together the stepfamily members and for keeping them together. Chapter Eight is about the experience of the couple in the center of a complex stepfamily system. At a time when most new couples would be enjoying their newfound companionship and getting to know each other, remarried couples are coping with children in transition, former spouses, and conflicting loyalties. It is easy to neglect the couple relationship. To do so, however, is to put the whole stepfamily in jeopardy. The couple's relationship with each other is often what makes the enterprise worthwhile.

In Chapter Nine we look at an even bigger picture, that of the divorced-remarried family. The two households in which the children reside and visit are linked no matter how friendly or hostile the adults feel and act toward each other. The relationships between the adults in this larger family change over time and can make a big difference in the functioning of each separate stepfamily.

A new baby is the topic of Chapter Ten. Making the decision to have a child is complicated when one or both partners are already parents. The new child can help to bind a family together. It can also stir up old jealousies and new resentments. Couples must learn to balance attachment to the new child and to the older children. Couples who cannot have children together, or choose not to, often mourn the loss of the "love child" that could have been theirs.

Finally, in Chapter Eleven, we meet six families who have experienced divorce and remarriage. We learn about the various changes that have occurred within them. These families demonstrate how the different minifamilies and parts of the divorced-remarried family affect each other as they develop. In some of the families changes take place relatively smoothly; in others the parents and children have problems. Sometimes the changes brought about by the remarriage are helpful in resolving their problems.

SUMMING UP

Living in a stepfamily is often difficult and painful. It can also help you to become a better, more understanding, more compassionate person. You and your children can learn to live with people who are not just like you. You can work out differences and learn to care about more people in your expanded family. You can have good times and become resources for one another. It is my hope in writing this book that you will use some of it to help your stepfamily along the road to understanding and affection. There is a great deal of love and hope in each of us. We need each other to bring it out.

CHAPTER TWO

The Divorcing Couple

Divorce hurts. You were in the habit of turning to your husband or wife with your hurts and loneliness. Now you are no longer there for each other. You may feel strange not giving each other comfort. You feel the weight of your history together urging you to listen one more time or try once again to explain yourself. You also hear your partner's words telling you it's over or your voice telling him it's over. When a marriage is becoming a divorce, you have to make drastic changes in the ways that you treat each other.

A common error of many divorcing couples is to assume that their relationship will soon be over completely. You keep waiting for the day when you will not wake up thinking about the person you are divorcing. That day will come, but not for months or even years after the initial separation.

Even though the marriage has ended, most former spouses continue to have relationships with each other for several years thereafter. Many concerned relatives and friends, as well as some professional helpers, consider a lingering attachment to the former wife or husband a sign of weakness or poor mental health. Recent research in this area, however, has pointed out that this is not necessarily so. In fact, in a study of 200 divorced men and women, nearly half felt they would have wanted to continue with the relationship with the former spouse even if there had been no children present.[1] For most couples, the children are the reason for their ongoing contact.

The formerly married couple are the two members of the former-spouse minifamily. Their minifamily, which is another description of the ways in which they continue to treat each other after the divorce, is a powerful part of the stepfamily (or stepfamilies) that will be created by the remarriage of one or both of them. The way in which the divorce and the changes that accompany it are handled directly affect the development of the stepfamily. That is why a book on stepfamilies must talk about divorce.

THE DIVORCING COUPLE

The goal of a married couple is to be close to each other. The goal of a divorcing couple is to move away from each other. This sudden about-face is slowed down by the ambivalence most people have about ending a marriage. Remember, most separations are preceded by months, or even years, of unhappiness or of trying to make a failing marriage work.

After the initial separation, both partners usually go through a period of holding on to the past. Each of you may still have hope that the marriage can be saved. Constant review of the events of the last few months, or the years of the entire marriage, is a frequent late-night or early-morning activity. As you try to sleep, you find yourself wondering what would have happened, "If only I hadn't criticized his mother so much" or "If only I hadn't lost that last job." The question is, Would you still be together?

During the stage of holding on you may still act in some of the ways you did when you were married, even though you and your mate are now living apart. Why not do your laundry in the washer and dryer you bought and installed in the basement of *your* house? Why not make an extra loaf of bread for your husband (after all, you're not divorced yet)?

After some time of holding on, you reach the stage of letting go. This is a time of accepting the end of the marriage and pushing away from the other person as hard as you dare. Anger flares up frequently. Unspoken accusations rise and are aired. You may wonder what you have done to deserve such temper tantrums from your estranged husband or wife. Probably nothing out of the ordinary. It is part of the process that must occur for an emotional divorce to take place. Don't be shocked when you find yourself stamping your feet like a two-year-old. You won't always be angry and neither will he or she.

When you let go, you also stop taking care of the other person. Even though you may still care about your former spouse's welfare, you are no longer responsible for fixing her car or making sure he has curtains in his new apartment. One man who had recently separated from his wife spent a fall weekend patching the roof of the house they still owned together. The next weekend he drove to the house to make more repairs, looked at it from his car window, and left. He reached his new apartment, called his wife, and told her to find someone else to fix "her" roof.

The husband and wife can reach the holding-on and letting-go stages at different times. A woman described a phone call from her husband, from whom she had been separated for six months. "He called last night to say he's being laid off. He was real upset. I tried to think, if I was being fired, would I call him about it? And I have to honestly say, no."

Many people feel it would be easier to get over the divorce if they did not have to see each other when they did not want to. Parents who are attempting to share the care of their children, and this is the growing trend of the 1980s, cannot avoid each other. One mother described her frustration. "I had a real nice talk with Tony [her ex-husband] the other night about Donny [her son] and how he'll do in kindergarten. Tony and I were talking without fighting for the first time in months. Then, as I was leaving, he says, 'What are you doing tomorrow night? Want to have dinner?' This drives me crazy. He keeps trying to get me to move back in." This woman had let go of her husband while he was still holding on.

If you are in a relationship with someone who is getting divorced, you may have wondered why he or she did not make a "clean break" from his or her spouse. There is no such thing as a clean break. Divorce is messy. For some time after the divorce, entanglements with the past seem never-ending. Eventually, however, formerly married couples learn to let go; they both reach the third stage of divorce, that of starting over, and they are each freer to care for others.

Marriage is a source of identity. It gives us a way of defining who we are. This definition continues in the stages of holding on and letting go. One woman when asked by a friend how she was, replied, "I'm divorced." In the stage of starting over, you begin to find other sources of identity and self-esteem. Starting over is a time when you learn to put yourself first, to take care of you, to make your own plans and to be a parent in your own way.

By this time, you know the marriage cannot be reconciled. You know you can survive on your own, as a single parent or a parent whose children visit. Somehow you're making ends meet, though it may be just barely. You no longer have to give in to the demands of your ex-wife or ex-husband out of fear, loneliness, or habit.

Saying no to your former mate is not easy, but it becomes a necessary part of defining your own personality and your own needs.

"No, I can't keep the kids till 10 o'clock on Sunday night so you can go to a movie. Get a baby-sitter."

"No, I can't loan you my Aunt Sarah's quilt even if it would look nice in your new study."

"I came to pick up the kids. I can't give you a ride to the Mobil station to pick up your car."

Your ex-wife or ex-husband is likely to feel hurt, angry, or disappointed when you say no; but in the long run you are helping him or her. He has to learn to get baby-sitters. She has to find other rides, to broaden her resources beyond you. If she hasn't started by now, this is the time. You must take care of yourselves separately.

STARTING OVER

Most people muddle through the holding-on and letting-go stages of their divorced lives and arrive at starting over, ready to build new lives for themselves. For some the process takes a year; for others five years. You may struggle through it bravely on your own; your neighbor may need to join two support groups and phone her sister in Minneapolis twice a week for encouragement. Probably, neither one of you is aware that you have used an informal strategy for getting where you are or that you could purposely develop other strategies to change your situation.

We know what a strategy is on the battlefield, in a football game, or in a campaign to raise funds for the school library. What is a strategy in a family or in your personal life? It's a plan that takes into account the big picture (what we call the family as a system), the personalities involved, and the history of the situation. Most important, a strategy has a clear and attainable goal, a goal you can state in very precise terms. Although the overall goal of a football team is to win, the play-by-play goals may be to gain yardage or to block a particular player. Your overall goal may be to get through your divorce and be happy or to marry an attractive divorced woman and live peacefully with her and her children. These goals are too broad for planning strategies.

Let's look at a strategy for achieving one woman's short-term goal. "I want my ex-husband to stop calling me for help and advice on the Saturday nights that the children sleep at his house." If that was your goal, you might imagine some possible plans of action for achieving it:

1. Go out so you cannot answer the phone.
2. Stay home, but unplug the phone from the wall outlet.
3. Tell him not to call.
4. Tell the children you don't want him to call.
5. Invite a friend to your house. Have her answer the call and tell him you cannot come to the phone.
6. Invite your teenaged cousin to come. Have her answer the phone and talk to your ex-husband nonstop for twenty minutes if he calls.
7. Buy a new record and listen to it with your teenager's earphones.

This list is just a start. You are always the best person to choose the right plan for yourself. You will probably reject number 4 because you don't want the children to be in the middle. Number 3 has probably been tried already and has not worked. You still have many other options.

Now you must think about the likely consequences of your choice. If you choose number 1, will you go out somewhere and have a miserable time? Will you feel manipulated if you have to leave your house merely to avoid the phone calls from your ex-husband? If so, eliminate this one. If you choose number 2, will you be able to tolerate wondering whether the children are all right and whether he is really managing without you? That is most likely how you have been hooked all along. Changing his behavior means forcing yourself to act as if you trust him to care for the children and believing that the children can survive without you. For most mothers, and many fathers, this is extremely difficult. Nonetheless, you cannot have independence from your former husband unless you give him a chance. If you choose number 2, you might invite a friend to keep you company and be available in case you change your mind. If you do change your mind, she can answer the phone.

So far you have defined a problem and a goal, listed possible plans for achieving your goal, and chosen a strategy for a given night or series of nights. The next step is to know when you have achieved success. One Saturday night out—or with your phone unplugged—will not necessarily teach your husband not to call. It may take four weeks. You must allow time for changes to take place. Moreover, you must recognize that one call from him is better than five; although the call is still annoying, progress is evident. Once you choose a strategy, you have to stick with it for a while and evaluate change over time. You must also be flexible. If you send your eight-year-old to his father's with a temperature of 102 degrees and an ear infection, you may want to call to see how he's feeling.

Let's suppose your strategy works. Now what? You should congratulate yourself on taking more control of your live and on taking a step toward becoming a graduate of the divorce process. You are also freer to form a new relationship, knowing your Saturday nights won't be interrupted by frequent calls. Don't be surprised, however, if you also feel a bit sad and empty. After all, the calls for help and the plan to eliminate them filled up your Saturday nights alone. Now you must face yourself—and your own future. You are left with the sweet-and-sour task of once again making a life for yourself, whether it is alone, with friends, or with a new mate. You are freer to move on, but the freedom is not far from loneliness.

A word of caution is in order for the New Person. If your new friend is having trouble with a former spouse, you may have a strategy for change that you would like to suggest. Don't. You are likely to create a situation in which you yourself become the target of angry and hurt feelings.

Suppose it is your lover whose husband is calling every Saturday night to ask about bedtimes, baths, and pajamas. You feel annoyed that she is ignoring you while she advises the man who divorced her. You can gently ask her if the calls bother her. You can jokingly say you will hide the telephone in a closet. You can express frustration at her lack of interest in you. However, you cannot make her stop answering the phone calls. She must be ready to do this herself. When she asks for advice, you can state your plan. If the situation continues and she doesn't seem to want to be less involved with her ex-husband, she may not be as ready to have a relationship with you as she appears. Many recently divorced or divorcing people end new relationships because they are not ready to become involved with someone new and leave the marriage behind. The physical and even legal realities of separation and divorce may be far ahead of the emotional realities of letting go and starting anew.

COPARENTING

"Coparenting" is a term created to describe the relationship of a divorced couple who continue to share the care of their common children. It describes an ideal, final, outcome of the couple's divorce. They are no longer husband and wife, no longer adversaries in the divorce process, but coparents, two individuals connected to each other by concern for their children.

As coparents you can be civil, even friendly. You do not, however, have a relationship that goes beyond caring for the children. The former mates no longer have a sexual relationship, play racquetball, or host a party together. They may see each other on the Little League field, at school plays, and at pick up and delivery times for the children.

It generally takes several years before this relationship can become calm and businesslike. Before this time, though the subject of a conversation may be the children's summer schedule, the emotional aftermath of the divorce is always present. Your ex-wife changes her vacation plans, and you flash back on her flakiness when you were married. Your ex-husband won't give you a definite response, and you remember how he kept you guessing in the past.

Couples who have joint custody, or schedules with frequent visitation, may have a harder time getting along. The father who sees his children only twice a month has fewer reasons to interact with his ex-wife, and they often get on with their own lives more easily. Although less contact is easier on the parents, the children are happier and more secure when they see both parents regularly and frequently.

There are times when it's hard to draw the line between being a good parent and helping your ex-spouse. One father had arranged for his daughter, who lived in another town with her mother, to attend the superior school in his own neighborhood. When his ex-wife's car broke down and she couldn't afford to buy a new one, he reluctantly agreed to give her his old car. He knew his daughter appreciated the better school, but he resented giving his ex-wife a car that she would use for her own needs as well as their daughter's.

Getting used to being a coparent with the person who was your wife or husband is a hard feat. It requires patience, stamina, and creativity. You can make it easier by setting guidelines for yourself and your ex-spouse. Some people find it easier to talk on the phone than in person; some couples arrange for a special time each week to talk about the "business" of coparenting. The less you bring up subjects of conflict in front of the children, the happier they will be with both of you.

Harriet W. Lee, family law counselor and professor of law, suggests modeling the coparent relationship on a business partnership:

- Be businesslike with your former spouse. Test all of your own behavior against this standard: Was I businesslike?

- Test your ex-spouse's behavior not by how you feel but by the same standard. Was his or her behavior businesslike?

- Respect your children's relationship with your ex-spouse. Your children did not divorce either parent; don't force them to.

- Make appointments to talk about business. Except for emergencies, call only during business hours or agreed-upon times. Always ask if the timing is convenient; if not, make an appointment for a time that is.

- Be polite. Do not use bad language or name-call. Do not try to conduct business under the influence of alcohol or other drugs. If you feel yourself getting unbusinesslike, say so and agree to resume the conversation at a later time.

- Give the benefit of the doubt as to behavior, as you would with a stranger. Do not assume anything based on past experience without checking out now, at this time, reasons for behavior, what your partner thinks, or what your parenting partner has decided.

- Do not expect approval from your partner. Have your personal and emotional needs fulfilled elsewhere and with others.
- Do not discuss matters irrelevant to business unless your partner specifically agrees to do so. Respect your ex's privacy.
- Make all agreements explicit and follow up with written confirmation when possible (or make your own written memorandum). Be clear and complete in your communications.
- Keep agreements. Do not break appointments.
- Do not make unilateral decisions; consult your partner and the children so that the best and most workable decision can be made.
- Don't insist on what does not work.
- Above all, cultivate goodwill in the partnership. Keep in mind always the importance of your investment and the expected returns. The investment is what you are willing to do for your children's happiness and success in life. The returns are comfort and security for your children, and the knowledge that their parents care enough to make life work.[2]

ENTER THE NEW PERSON

Most people who get divorced are looking for new partners to love. Nearly 80 percent of those who are divorced do remarry. Others live together without marrying, and still others are looking for new partners. Being in a couple again helps us feel loved and lovable. It helps to remove some of the doubts about whether the divorce was "all my fault." It returns a sense of joy and brightness to life.

The New Person in your life (this person is not yet a stepparent and may not go on to become one) can also help you become less connected to your former wife or husband. When you meet this New Person, you have to cope with the continuing relationship with your ex-spouse as well as your new relationship.

At the very beginning of a new relationship you may not want to tell your former spouse about the New Person. The children are ready on the front porch when their father arrives Sunday afternoon to take them out. He looks surprised, lingers as though wondering why you're not inviting him in for coffee, as you often do. You don't tell him about the man who is having an after-lunch cigarette in your dining room.

As you become more involved in new relationships, you are less available to your former mate as a friend and adviser. You may have more reasons to change plans or to want a clear schedule for visitation times. John found his divorced life lonely and empty; he looked forward to seeing his children on weekends. He never refused his ex-wife's requests to switch weekends or take the children for an extra night. When he started dating Suzanne, however, he liked knowing they could spend a whole weekend without his children. The next time his ex-wife asked for weekend exchange, it would have meant missing a barbecue Suzanne had planned or taking his children to meet her (which he wasn't ready to do). He had to say no to his ex-wife and receive her angry response.

As the new relationship progresses, you may move away from your former spouse in additional ways. It's more pleasant to talk with the New Person about the children; you're more likely to agree. As one remarried mother of two boys said, "We agree on most things that come up with the boys. I think that Sandy [new spouse] and I agree more than Oscar [former husband] and I ever did. In fact, I wouldn't have married him if we didn't. I watched him with the boys for two years when we were dating."

THE NEWS

Telling your former wife or husband that you are involved with someone else is a task that needs a special strategy. You may not think your love life is any of his or her business or you may not think he or she will be upset by the news. That is just not true. You may think you can mention it in passing or let the children communicate the news. Sometimes this works. However, if you think carefully about how to share this information in a considerate and sensitive way, you will be repaid in cooperation and goodwill. The appropriate approach differs in each case. You must consider how long you have been divorced, how well you communicate, and what the implications are for your future coparenting. If your former wife lives down the street, is very dependent on you for child support, and has dinner with you every Wednesday, you may want to drop a few hints and then tell her in a way that is planned but looks casual. On the other hand, if your ex-husband has a full social life of his own and doesn't even look at you when he ushers the kids into his car every other week, you may just say, "Don't be surprised if the children are talking about a guy named Ron. He's someone I've been spending a lot of time with lately."

Surprises in this area are not appreciated. Slipping a few snapshots of you and your new friend, arm in arm, into a bunch of pictures you took of the children on vacation is not a great idea. Neither is sending your new friend to pick up the children at your husband's because you have a headache.

Suppose you had been seeing someone secretly for several months before you left the house. Waiting several more months to bring up the subject of this New Person may be concealing something, but it will also protect you from many accusations and allow the New Person the possibility of developing a good relationship with your children and being treated civilly by your former husband. Your ex-spouse may wonder just how long you have known each other, but he is unlikely to ask.

A strategy that allows some time to elapse between the first mention of your new relationship and the time you expect your ex and the New Person to meet is wise. Don't call on Sunday morning to announce that you have met a fabulous woman and she is coming to help you pack up the books you left in the den.

What happens if you all meet suddenly and inadvertently? Your former husband may assume that you are dating, but he can still be upset by seeing you in line at the movie theater holding hands with another man. If this happens, make the meeting as brief and casual as possible; all three of you may be very uncomfortable. It is not the time to engage your ex-husband in a long conversation about your son's hockey league.

You may find yourself surprisingly distressed when you learn that your former partner is in a new relationship. Like many other people, you criticize yourself for not taking the news more casually. You may not want to have your ex-spouse back, but you are not unusual if you feel hurt and jealous when you know he or she is seeing somebody else.

You may also be jealous because he or she is in a relationship and you are not. As one woman said, "I'm fit to be tied. He's out on the town, and here I am still lonely and miserable. It's not fair. I wouldn't feel so bad if he were miserable, too."

If your former spouse mentions a New Person to you, you are not required to say anything more than "oh" or "that's nice." You may already have guessed from the comments of the children. It's better not to pump them for information. They usually dislike spying on one parent for the other; they have their own feelings to cope with. Moreover, their information is frequently inaccurate.

When you learn your former husband now has an "almost live-in" woman friend, you realize that he has been talking to you on the phone a lot less. You may feel that he is less available to you as a coparent or to the children. Parents frequently complain that ex-spouses seem less interested in sharing information about the children once they are in new relationships. If you are not in a relationship of your own, it's hard not to feel left out and let down. You miss the adult contact. Your coparent has another adult to share with and you don't.

There are also times when your life as a divorced person with children is made more complicated and difficult because your children's other parent is in a new relationship. You may dislike changing your plans so your ex-husband can be with Valerie for her birthday. You resent giving up a weekend visit with your son so that his mother and Steve can take him camping with them. You don't like hearing your ex-husband complain about the expense of the baby-sitters he hires so he can go out with Lois.

You may feel that this New Person is influencing your former spouse to treat the children differently or inappropriately. One woman's new friend convinced her to put her TV in the attic and have her children read for an hour every night. The children's father was incensed that he could do nothing to change her mind. He let the children watch unlimited TV at his house to compensate. His ex-wife became furious with him in return.

THE TRIANGLE

We often refer to the relationship between the three adults—the couple who used to be married and the new partner of one of them—as a triangle. It is more like a tug-of-war. One person is in two relationships, and any communications between the other two go through him or her.

Nelson, the divorced father of three children, was often teased by his friends for being Mr. Nice Guy. After separating from his wife, Louise, he continued to take his children out every Sunday and to help Louise with a series of problems in her life.

One Sunday night he returned the children and found Louise sitting in a puddle on the kitchen floor trying to fix a leak under the kitchen sink. Nelson had already repaired that sink several times; he was quite handy. Louise was clearly expecting him to roll up his sleeves, get his toolbox from the car, and pitch in. Ordinarily he wouldn't have minded.

But that night he had someone in the car waiting to be taken out to dinner. Her name was Debbie and she was special. She was already dubious about dating a divorced father with three children. There was no way he could keep her waiting while he fixed a leak.

"You'll have to call a plumber," he said to Louise.

"But it's Sunday," she answered, looking surprised.

"I'll turn the water off in the kitchen for you."

"Look, you've fixed it before. It won't take long."

Nelson was moving toward the door. "Sorry, I've got to run."

"But it's your house, too." Louise was raising her voice.

"Sorry. I'm in a rush."

"With the money you give me, I can't afford a plumber."

By this time Louise was yelling, Nelson was feeling anxious about Debbie in the car, and the boys were throwing toy cars into the puddle to watch the splashes. Back in the car, Debbie wanted to know what took so long.

All evening Nelson was haunted by guilty feelings. How could he have left Louise with all that mess and the three kids to get to bed? Would she calm down enough to check Billy's homework and soak Tim's infected toe? He doubted it. He couldn't share his concerns with Debbie, either.

This is a simple story, hardly of any significance, you might think. However, stepfamily life is a string of little stories, one after the other, in which one person is torn between two important others. Furthermore, this scenario illustrates the way in which the roles we play in our families influence how we feel and what we think. Nearly anyone in one of these roles would react similarly to Louise, Nelson, or Debbie.

Louise could not understand why Nelson would be so inconsiderate. What had gotten into him? He wasn't acting like himself. In her anger, she found herself thinking of ways to pay him back for his cruelty. When the children were cranky, she told them they were just like their father and called him names, something she had vowed she would never do. If she had known that Debbie was waiting in the car, she would have understood Nelson's behavior, but she might have been even angrier. "He's running off to party while I clean up this mess."

Debbie wondered why Nelson, who left the car in a cheerful mood, had returned looking so glum. She didn't ask because she didn't know much about divorce and she didn't want to pry. When his distraction continued throughout the evening, she began to wonder if she was boring him. Perhaps he was sorry he had invited her; perhaps he didn't like her as much as she liked him. If Debbie had known what happened in Louise's kitchen, she might have felt that the problem was all her fault. If she hadn't come, Louise would have a working sink and Nelson would not feel guilty. She might have also been angry that Louise even existed and that her evening had to be spoiled by another woman's problems.

Nelson was truly caught between his loyalty to Louise, his responsibility within the former-spouse minifamily, and his desire to have a new relationship. His needs and Louise's needs were in direct conflict. He chose his own needs. He was moving into the stage of starting over, and saying no to Louise was important for his growth. Knowing that Debbie, too, was counting on him helped him say no. Putting himself first was different from what he did in most situations in his life. He didn't feel like himself.

Some discomfort with making a new choice in a familiar situation is normal for everyone. Change rarely comes without pain. The fact that Nelson could have some compassion for Louise at the same time that he chose to take care of his own evening showed a sensitivity that was probably a quality Debbie liked in him.

Our Sunday night scene also demonstrates how a family works as a system. Remember how confusing the baseball game is when we don't know the rules? If we look at this scene with no prior information, we don't understand why Debbie had to wait in the car while the others went in. We don't know why Louise expected Nelson to fix something in her home. The piece of information that can help us make sense of what we see is the strength of the former-spouse minifamily. Debbie, as an outsider to this minifamily, was not welcome in their former home. The minifamily history accounts for Louise's expectations that Nelson would help her and Nelson's guilt about not helping.

We also gain some understanding about minifamilies. The Nelson-and-Louise minifamily was more than Nelson plus Louise. It included their history, their expectations, and their way of doing things. Just as people behave differently in a church, a bar, at the office, or on the beach, individuals act differently according to the minifamily or family of which they are a part.

The system of Nelson, Louise, and Debbie also had certain rules. Debbie, though a friendly woman who would have offered sympathy and help to a friend in Louise's situation, was not able to reach out to Louise. Nelson had to choose between the appropriate action for the former-spouse minifamily or the minifamily-in-formation with Debbie. Within this setup, someone had to be disappointed, just as in the baseball game, one team has to be the winner and one the loser. The Red Sox pitcher may have been best friends with the Yankee first baseman before he was traded. Now he tries his best to strike out his old friend. Similarly, Louise and Debbie might have liked each other if they had worked together in the same office, but they were resentful of each other in their roles with Nelson.

The roles we play within a family have tremendous power over us. Within them, we become loyal, prejudiced, and competitive. We also learn the ways the other players react. If you have a funny feeling in your stomach that your ex-husband is going to yell at you when he sees that you have taken his parents' portrait off the mantel, you are probably right. When we plan our strategies, we must take into account knowledge of what the system does as well as our familiarity with the individuals. Louise thought she knew Nelson from cover to cover, but she did not know that he was acting as a new date to someone else and that, within that context, he would behave differently with her.

Understanding these powerful forces, however, does not mean we have to be ruled by them. Many people are happy in their second marriages precisely because they have been able to go beyond the rules and expectations that they originally had. The Debbies and Louises learn to give each other a break; the Nelsons learn how to share their feelings.

Over 1 million families are divorcing each year in this country.[3]

Of these, 60 percent have children under the age of eighteen.[4] Four marriages in ten are second marriages for one or both parties.[5] Thus, each year millions of families are entering or continuing stepfamily life. There are some rules, patterns, and experiences that they all have in common.

The rules and expectations for stepfamilies are different from those for nuclear families. Some situations that would seem outrageous if you were still married are considered normal after divorce or remarriage. For example, you are sitting at your son's graduation. To your left is your son's father, to his left is his second wife, and to your right is the second wife's daughter, who likes you.

In stepfamilies we are also faced with decisions we never would have anticipated. Denise received a small inheritance from her Aunt Martha. Three years before she would have called Robert at his office and suggested a celebration. Now, divorced from him, she doesn't want to tell him about it. She fears it will give him a reason to stop sending child support checks. Is she right to keep this a secret?

Sunday is Spenser's day to see the children. His ex-wife, Shirley, thinks he has an obligation to take the children out every Sunday so she can have a day off. Spenser thinks he has the privilege of visiting his children on the Sundays he chooses, when he has no conflicting plans. Who is right?

Your own response to these touchy questions will be strongly influenced by your situation. If you are a divorced mother, you will most likely sympathize with Denise. The inheritance is extra, something for a special occasion or an emergency. If you are a divorced father paying child support, you probably think she is dishonest not to share the information. After all, Robert was probably kind to Aunt Martha all the years of his marriage. Why shouldn't his load be made easier by her bequest?

Here is a very important exercise. In your mind, try switching roles. If you are a Denise, try being Robert for five minutes. Can you imagine how he feels, what he thinks, what he would like to say to you? Can you feel the anger, the pain, or the old love? Now trying switching roles with your own ex-spouse or the ex-spouse of your partner. If you are a Debbie or a Louise (or a Dick or a Louis), can you feel what it would be like to be in the other position?

Learning to take another person's point of view can help you in two ways. First, it can make you more sympathetic to the other people in your stepfamily system. Second, it can help you in planning your strategies because you can predict their responses to your actions.

HOW THE NEW PERSON HELPS THE FORMER SPOUSES TO SEPARATE

Although the postdivorce family system often puts the New Person in competition with the former spouse for the time and attention of the dating spouse, the New Person can also take some pressure off the former spouse. One man was delighted that his former wife had someone else to help her with her taxes. Another was pleased that his children's mother was more cheerful since she had met another man. A divorced mother was relieved that her ex-husband stopped making passes at her once he had a new woman friend. If you have been feeling guilty about leaving your ex, you may sigh with relief once he or she is hooked up with a New Person.

One mother was grateful that her children were returned home from their visits with clean hands, clean clothes, and brushed hair whenever their father's new friend came along with them. Another woman received a Mother's Day card from her five-year-old son for the first time in the three years since her divorce. It was clear that the new woman had helped the boy select and mail the card, but the mother nonetheless felt less angry toward her ex-husband now that she was receiving more recognition for her role. In the first several years after a separation it is awkward going to the same place as your former spouse: your child's ball game, a potluck supper with his Scout troop, or her performance in a school play. If you are by yourself, you may not want to sit next to your former spouse. You may also feel strange sitting by yourself. When one of you brings a New Person for the first time, it is embarrassing; but it is also clear that you no longer have to pretend to be friendlier than you are. You become separate in the public eye as well as in your private lives.

THE REMARRIAGE

The remarriage of a divorced spouse is a big step in making the divorce more definitive and in limiting the former-spouse minifamily to coparenting. Even the person who is remarrying may feel a touch of sadness about the former marriage that did not work out. (Don't share this with your new wife or husband on the eve of your wedding.)

When your former partner is getting married again, you may worry about his or her commitment to your children and to staying in touch with you. Will the new marriage be all-consuming? Will her new husband get a job in another state and take your former wife and your children along? Will your ex-husband keep up his support checks? These worries reflect the deeper meaning of the second marriage. The former spouse, while remaining your ex-husband or your ex-wife, is now also someone else's present spouse. He or she has strong ties and responsibilities to that new spouse.

In fact, many parents do communicate less frequently with their former spouses after remarriage. Some do see their children less or have other stepchildren in their lives to care for. However, remarriage rarely interferes with a divorced parent's basic commitment to or love for his or her children.

The person who is not getting married often feels lonely and excluded at the time of the wedding. The children are usually invited, and you may be asked to drive them there or pick them up. The wedding is one of the first major family events to which you have not been invited. You may feel hurt when your former in-laws, in town for the wedding, do not call you. If you are about to be the nonmarrying partner, you might consider planning something special for yourself. It's better to have a pleasant distraction or a weekend with old friends than to be miserable or put yourself down when you cannot stop thinking about "their" wedding.

THE AFFAIR

Having an affair is a special way of ending a marriage. Although many people who separate from their spouses are involved in extramarital affairs at the time of the separation or shortly thereafter, very few of these relationships become remarriages. When they do, however, there are many extra problems in the former-spouse minifamily.

One difficulty is that the decision to divorce is often made quickly and without ample consideration. Although marriages can survive the affairs of one or both partners, many people assume that lipstick on the collar means that divorce court is the next step.

When Nicole's husband discovered that she was having an affair with her boss, he pinned her to the wall and told her she had to choose between the other man and her child. In a panic at his rage and frightened by his violence, Nicole left the house and moved in with her boss without thinking about whether she really was ready to end her marriage and leave her two-year-old. She felt she had let herself get caught misbehaving and, like a naughty child, she had to take the consequences, which included losing custody of her daughter. Looking back several years later, she realized that she had been unhappy in her marriage but hadn't known how to talk to her husband about it. She had become involved in the extramarital affair as a distraction. The affair started out as her way of telling her husband that she was not happy. It turned into the reason for a divorce.

An affair occurs in a marriage that is already in trouble, whether or not the husband and wife are willing to face it. The affair is a distraction from existing problems. Sometimes the person left out is relieved to have the other person "working late" or staying out at "late meetings." The partner who is having the affair may become easier to live with until the whole thing blows up. Then the hurt and anger of the person being deceived are usually so great that he or she is unable to discuss the marital problems or accept any of the responsibility for the marriage not working out.

It is easy and tempting to blame the "other woman" or "other man" for wrecking the marriage. A deserted partner feels more comfortable assuming that an evil but attractive other person stole the spouse away rather than recognizing that the spouse has been dissatisfied for a long time. The partner having the affair often blames the former spouse for being such a poor mate that he or she had to seek love and understanding somewhere else. This mutual blaming can go on for years and certainly does not end with the remarriage of one partner or the other.

A couple who divorce under these circumstances never have a chance to say good-bye without the shadow of the New Person hanging over them. The person who is leaving for someone else may feel disloyal to the New Person if he or she expresses any positive feelings toward the former mate. Morever, one kind word to the deserted spouse is often mistaken for encouragement to keep waiting for the partner's return.

The spouse left behind often feels enormous rage and wants retribution. The person leaving often feels guilty and is willing to give in to the former spouse on many demands but cannot give unlimited aid, money, or time.

The person who is not remarrying is forced to cope with two major changes at once—the ending of a marriage and the beginning of a stepfamily for the former spouse and children. You have barely accepted the separation that has taken place when your husband turns into the driveway with "her" in the car. You are still wondering whether your wife will come back to you, and then she announces that she's going to Nassau for a week with "him."

It is easy to lose all trust in the former spouse who has had the affair. The partner left behind has had little choice about ending the marriage. His or her sense of powerlessness may be expressed through angry and extreme demands, lack of cooperation in co-parenting, or bizarre and unpredictable behavior. The "other" person becomes a symbol of all the pain of the divorce. Sometimes it is years before the spouse left behind can call the new partner by name, speak to him or her on the phone, and not be angry that the children are spending time with "that person."

Another pattern develops in this setup that definitely affects the new stepfamily: The person having the affair becomes accustomed to keeping secrets. He or she develops a pattern of dealing with conflict through avoidance. After the remarriage, he or she is likely to continue withholding information that may cause anger or conflict. Patty's ex-husband, Ron, told her that his father was very ill and he might have to leave town suddenly if his father's condition worsened. Patty, hoping for the best, said nothing to her new husband. During the children's next visit, however, Ron was called to his father's deathbed. He dropped the children at Patty's on his way to the airport. She was not surprised to see them because she had been forewarned. Her husband was angry at not being told that this change might happen. He couldn't understand why his wife had not shared the information with him. She explained that she hadn't wanted to upset him in case the children were not brought home early.

This situation, marriage-affair-divorce-remarriage, is another one in which the system sets people against each other. The "other" woman or man is often a charming, kind, and sensitive person who happens to fall in love with someone who is in an unsatisfying marriage. Often the married person gives the lover only partial information or says, "I've been planning to move out for a long time. I'm not doing it for you." The New Person may also be divorced and may even feel some sympathy toward the spouse being left behind. Although the two men or the two women may have a lot in common, and may or could have been friends before the divorce, they usually become silent enemies.

IN CONCLUSION

Ending a marriage is never easy or pleasant. In any case, both of you often feel sad, angry, and abandoned. Rarely is anyone completely healed from the pain of the divorce before meeting another person to whom he or she wants to be close. Most of us use a new relationship as one way of getting over the hurt, of feeling lovable again, and of moving on with our lives.

The stepfamily has its beginnings in the ending of the first marriage for one or both partners. You cannot leave the past entirely behind you. Understanding what you and your partner bring with you helps both of you to be patient, to suggest changes, and to build the best possible stepfamily for yourselves and your children.

CHAPTER THREE
Parenting after Divorce

Your marriage is over. You're coming out of your state of shock. You're single again. You start to remember what it was like to be single, and your reverie is interrupted by a baby's cry, the sound of children arguing, or a phone call from your teenager. Being single before marriage did not involve parenting.

The children remain part of your life. You may blame them for the divorce or feel grateful that you still have a family. You may see them seven days a week or only seven days a year. Whether they are nasty, loving, condescending, cheerful, or exasperating, they are your children. They do not go up in smoke when your marriage does. They need you, and you will discover that you need them.

Parenting after a separation is extremely stressful. While you are questioning the changes in your identity, you are confronted with children who clamor for your attention, challenge your authority, and barely give you a chance to catch your breath. A common reaction on experiencing the pain, confusion, and self-doubts of separation is to assume that things will *never* get any better. Time loses its meaning. Each moment is a major undertaking. Fortunately, the chaos eventually resolves into a new form of order.

Children's needs do not change drastically after a divorce, but the form of your family does. The changes in the family form, or structure, affect your behavior, your children's behavior, and even the behavior of a new friend or lover who you hope will someday be a stepparent to your children.

CHILDREN'S UNDERSTANDING OF DIVORCE

A young child's view of reality is essentially egocentric. A three-year-old thinks it snows so she can go sledding. An eight-year-old thinks his angry feelings toward his younger brother caused the brother's broken leg. Only at adolescence does the child's reasoning process begin to resemble an adult's.

Young children often think relationships exist as a result of physical proximity. (Blake is my buddy because he lives next door.) With this cognitive framework, they have a difficult time understanding how a parent who moves out can remain a loving parent to them.

Children do not distinguish between their parents as parents and their parents as husband and wife to each other. They barely distinguish one parent's feelings or point of view from the other's. Mommy-and-Daddy is a solid unit. They also have trouble separating their own feelings from those of the parent. Is it okay for me to love Daddy even if Mommy doesn't love him? Can Daddy love me even if he doesn't love Mommy?

In the first year after the marital separation, the child has certain emotional work to do that is different from the emotional work of the parent. This table demonstrates the differences:

EMOTIONAL TASKS OF CHILD AND PARENT FOLLOWING DIVORCE

Child	*Parent*
Overcome grief and sadness	Overcome grief and anger
Make sense of new kind of family	Move away from former spouse
Keep up relationship with mother	Move from holding on to letting go
Keep up relationship with father	Keep minifamily going
Grow intellectually, physically, and emotionally	Repair and maintain self-esteem
Gain or maintain sense of self	Prepare for new relationships

Your child's focus is on keeping up the relationship with each parent. Your focus, as an adult, is on reaching a state of equilibrium in your relationships with your ex-spouse and your children so that you can move on to a new relationship.

MINIFAMILIES AFTER DIVORCE

After a divorce, the family carries on its child-rearing activities in two separate households. You move from sharing a prime-time news show to reporting solo on two competing channels. Instead of saying, "Here's Sally with tonight's sports," you are covering news, sports, weather, features, and finances. You and your competitor differ in your interpretations of the day's events, in your style and your opinions. You are trying to attract the same audience, your kids. As long as you attempted to stay married, you were inclined to cover up differences or give in to your partner. Now that you're on your own, you are more likely to express your individuality.

Each parent becomes a generalist rather than a specialist. This is a necessity with young children who need nearly constant care—feeding, dressing, bathing, comforting, and watching. Older children can wait to get their needs met, and each parent can provide some unique resources. Nonetheless, the feeling that you are "it" can be overwhelming. You can't go out in the driveway and play catch with your daughter while your wife makes dinner. If your son needs to go to the doctor for stitches, you have to take the other children along. If your teenage daughter goes baby-sitting on her weekend with you, you're the one she'll call when she can't get the baby to stop crying.

How can you adjust to this new routine? Here are some general suggestions:

1. Be patient. Change is always hard, and children resist it more than we do. Just when you think you'll never teach them to wash their hands before dinner, they may surprise you by remembering.
2. Get lots of help. Exhaust your relatives and friends. You may not be able to pay them back in kind, but you don't have to.

Many people feel good when they can help out, especially if they know you have been going through a rough time.

3. Take care of yourself. Find some ways to make your life easier and more pleasant. This might mean having pizza one night each week so you don't have to cook or spending one night a week at the gym getting your body in shape.

4. Don't be too hard on yourself. The last thing you need is another list of "shoulds" that you are not living up to. No one going through a divorce can be an ideal parent.

TIME WITH THE CHILDREN

Like most of us, you probably take your children for granted. You probably complain about them more than you praise them. In divorce negotiations, children become assets to be divided between two people. Time with them becomes a valuable commodity. You fight over the number of weekends you will see them and the privilege of having them for the holidays. Some couples argue about the exact hour of the pickup or return on the weekend. Many people struggle to have as much time with their children as they can, both to uphold their parental identity and to avoid losing the youngsters' affection.

Time without the children also becomes a treasured resource. Being totally in charge of your children for a week or a weekend is draining. Most divorced parents appreciate a break. In the beginning, you want time to cry or let yourself feel angry or depressed. Later on, you use that time to be social and single and to meet new people. You may discover that your new friends appreciate the childless time more than you do.

The attachment between children and parents, more than most other relationships, is grounded in being together in many different ways, rather than coming together for a special purpose. Giving up that general sense of connection and togetherness is painful. Divorced fathers often feel a sense of emptiness when they come home from work late and realize that they can't take a peek at their sleeping children. Custodial mothers who complain about the burden of single parenting would nevertheless rarely switch places with their former spouses. They value the experience of being with the children on a nearly daily basis.

If you are not divorced yourself, and if you are going out with someone who is, this emphasis on child time and nonchild time may seem puzzling at first. You are not used to planning outings on alternate weekends or needing permission from a third party, the children's other parent, before you can pack the children in the car and go to the beach. This is one fact of divorced-remarried life that requires some adjustment for everyone. Your partner has already had a chance to get used to this way of life, and you may be echoing some of his or her initial feelings that are now forgotten.

The more you try to offer support and understanding of your partner's real grief, the closer you will be able to become. There are also times when the best thing is to remind your partner that life goes on regardless of the children's presence or absence.

Initially, some divorced parents feel so genuinely lonely for their children and so guilty about the divorce that they do not allow themselves to have a good time with other adults. When Ruth, a newly separated mother of two girls, went away without them for the first time, to an ocean resort, she couldn't help missing them almost constantly.

"Wouldn't that be a good place for a sand castle?"

"This is the kind of shell Louise likes."

"Terry would love climbing these dunes."

She called her children five times in two days and bought several gifts for each of them. Luckily for Ruth, her friend had been through the same thing and understood what was happening. She consoled Ruth by reminding her of the many chances she would have to bring the children to the beach. She also emphasized the freedom she had as a childless adult, to use the health spa, to stay out late, and to sleep late in the morning.

THE CUSTODIAL MINIFAMILY

If you had to sum up the life of the single parent in one word, that word would be *overload*. The work of parenting and homemaking— usually in addition to part- or full-time work—is similar, but there is much more of it.

Most single parents are women, over 5.5 million in this country in 1983.[1] The custodial or single-parent household is the primary home of the children. When you become a single parent, you find that you must care for your children more of the time, with less help and less money. Moreover, your children have their own reasons for being harder to care for. The despair and pain of most recently separated parents is matched only by their courage and persistence in getting through the rough first few months.

The custodial minifamily undergoes a truly amazing evolution during the first year or two after the separation. Surviving the loss of one parent from the household requires many adjustments. A slow healing process, which is shared by parent and children, results in a new identity for the single-parent family. By the time of a remarriage, the minifamily members have usually become more stable, have developed clear ways of coping with the outside world, and have worked out new ways of relating to each other. This transformation, while necessary and creative for the minifamily in its development, is a barrier to the New Person who would like to enter the minifamily as a new member. Actually, the minifamily cannot absorb new members. A remarriage will mean the creation of a new family, of which the minifamily is only one part.

After separation the custodial minifamily develops a new boundary that differentiates it from other families and the previous family. Moving the former spouse—usually the father—to the outside of this boundary takes time. The children are likely to consider him a family member in absentia. He may even have a key to the house, which he uses when he drops the children off or picks them up at school and stops at the house to get their belongings.

Donald, for example, took his children out to dinner on Wednesday nights and returned them to Paula's house, where he put them to bed and baby-sat until Paula returned from her exercise class. This seemed like a convenient and inexpensive way to kill two birds with one stone—Donald's visit and Paula's night out. The children, however, wishing that Donald would move back in, took this weekly visit in their mother's home to mean that their father was still a family member. When Paula started using her Wednesday nights to have dinner with Greg, rather than going to exercise class, Donald's presence in her home was an embarrassment. It was clear that her little family of herself and two children had a "ghost" member who could make himself visible from time to time.

Financial independence is a fact we assume about a nuclear family. On the other hand, it is not uncommon for the single-parent mother to be dependent on her ex-husband, her parents, or the welfare department for part of her income. The financial arrangements can blur the boundary between the minifamily and whoever is providing financial support. A divorced mother does not want to bite the hand that feeds her children. She may give in to her ex-husband in order to ensure that the child support continues. If she receives welfare, she has to follow regulations and allow a welfare worker to enter her minifamily's home with questions and suggestions.

Moving back in with your parents sometimes seems like a way out of a financial and emotional quagmire. The rent-free abode, complete with built-in baby-sitter (your mom) and mechanic (your dad) has strong appeal as you struggle each day to get your kids to day care and yourself to work. The parent who chooses this solution often finds that her parents expect her to behave as she did when she was a teenager. They ask her where she's going, give her unsolicited advice, and try to take over the rearing of the children. They also try to form a boundary around the new two-generational family, which makes it hard for new partners to enter.

Stella was twenty-four when her husband moved out, leaving her with an infant and a three-year-old. She had been having trouble managing the two children even before the separation, and the idea of grandparental help was irresistible.

The first two months I was so exhausted I was just glad to have a bed to drop into and someone else to pick up the baby when she cried. I never slept more than two hours at a stretch during the night. I was a wreck. Then right after Jessie's birthday, I literally opened my eyes. My mother had invited her friends and their grandchildren to the birthday party. She didn't even consult me. I felt like a guest as my mother brought in the cake and my father started singing "Happy Birthday." Was this the way I wanted to live my adult life? That night I made a plan for getting a job, a cheap apartment, and some child care for my kids. It took another eight months, but now I'm on my own. I'm looking forward to dating, too. I could never have brought a new man home to my parents. They might start blinking the porch light like they did when I was a teenager necking with my boyfriend.

COPING

The first survival task of the single-parent family is to fill in for the absent parent. All the functions of that parent must now be done in other ways. The division of the missing parent's household, financial, and emotional responsibilities is not easy.

The single parent, usually the mother, often gets the lion's share of extra work. She has to work longer hours to earn more money, spend more nonworking time caring for the children, make more decisions on her own, and take care of basic household chores. She has to do all this without the emotional support and emergency backup of the other parent.

Some of the father's functions can be taken over by the children. They may do more chores or get part-time jobs. An older child may take on some fatherly responsibilities, teaching a younger child how to kick a soccer ball or providing help with homework.

The family must often depend on people outside their household as well. A neighbor or baby-sitter watches the children after school. A grandfather or uncle helps out with household repairs or with the children. A friend, counselor, or child's teacher becomes a confidant or gives the mother feedback about the children. The tasks once performed by one person within the family are now distributed among many others both inside and outside the family.

This was brought home dramatically to Alyson when she had to have another operation. At the time of her first operation, several years earlier, her husband had taken a week of vacation time to stay home with the children, visit her in the hospital, and keep the household going. Now he was not only out of the house but out of the picture. She had to rely on her mother for help the first weekend, on her neighbors to walk the children home from school, on baby-sitters to help her give them dinner and get them to bed each night. Her friends called her daily to be sure she had adults to talk with. Although she had nearly as much help as she needed, she felt that the task of arranging it all had been Herculean. Her biggest worry as the date of the surgery approached was not that something would go wrong medically but that one of the helpers she had lined up would not come through for her and the children.

In order to get through the operation, Alyson had to open up the boundaries of her minifamily to accept help of many sorts from her mother, her neighbors, and baby-sitters. Paradoxically, the experience also brought her and the children closer together. During the time she took off from work she was home many more hours than usual. Although she could not move around enough to get meals ready, prepare baths, or clean up, her presence was felt by the children. One of her sons even turned down a weekend invitation from his best friend in order to be close to his mother. When she could get around better, the children were proud of her.

As a minifamily, Alyson and her children had an unspoken feeling of satisfaction that they could manage without Dad. This sense of self-sufficiency, the result of Alyson's hard work and her children's consideration, will probably be an obstacle to a new man in Alyson's life when he wants to become a stepfather. Nonetheless, we cannot doubt that Alyson made the best choices under the circumstances.

MINIFAMILY CHANGES

The custodial minifamily changes in response to the divorce in several important ways.

Closeness

In their pain and confusion following a separation, children and parents often turn to each other for comfort and support. Your children, you discover, can be good companions. You stop rushing to put them to bed on time, an impossible task anyway. On the weekends, you all gather together and watch a movie on TV. You share popcorn and hot chocolate. When they are sad, you hold them, and your own tears flow more easily now as well. They cheer you up with jokes, distract you with mischief, and often seem to know what you are thinking or feeling before you do.

Discipline

As a lone parent it is harder to enforce all the rules. You don't have the backup of your partner; you're especially tired. You may give in more than you used to. In fact, research on divorced families has shown that discipline frequently loosens in the first year following separation and becomes more strict the year after that.[2]

The children become more powerful members of the family because you need them more. Their chores are not merely an exercise in character building, but a necessity in running the household. Their presence confirms the existence of the family. In your nuclear family when the eight-year-old threw his peas across the table and talked back to you, you may have sent him to his room so you and your wife could have a peaceful meal. Now, sending him to his room means eating alone. Moreover, because you are a visiting dad, it means giving up one of your three weekly meals together. You beg him not to throw his peas; you ignore him the first time he talks back. You give up some of your power in the family hierarchy in order to get along.

Sometimes guilt, plain and simple, gets the better of your common sense. You know Jeffie's already had too many sweets, but you can't refuse him an ice-cream pop before bed. You know a decent mother could make her kids clean up their own dirty laundry, but your kids have been through so much already. A dad should put his foot down when his ten-year-old daughter brings home four-letter words, but you don't have the heart to criticize her; you don't want to be the bad guy again. These changes are natural and painful. Sooner or later, you (or by that time, you and your new partner) will have to start the difficult task of undoing some bad habits.

If you are doubting your parenting abilities, just remember:

- Wrecking your children is harder than you think. Your presence and care for them, however inadequate it seems to you, is meaningful.
- Setting limits is a way of showing your love. "No" is as loving as "yes" if "no" means protecting your children and helping them grow.
- Giving in is not terrible on special occasions or when you are too exhausted to argue.
- Divorce is a process. You are going through stages, and so is your minifamily. What feels like a permanent state of chaos or confusion will change.

SWITCHING ROLES

Some divorced parents say, "When it comes to getting my life going again, I'm thirty-five going on sixteen and my daughter's sixteen going on thirty-five." If your children are teenagers, you may feel that the differences in your ages have become less important since the divorce. They are dating and so are you. They are having identity crises and so are you. They are confused and so are you. Sometimes the children start taking over not only the chores and responsibilities delegated to them by their parents but the authority of their parents as well. Beware. This may be a danger sign.

No matter how comforting it is to know your fourteen-year-old will be waiting up for you (and worrying) when you work late or date, it is not in her best interest to act as your parent. She needs to be involved in her own activities. Clearly, she is too old for a babysitter, but she may need company when you are out late.

It's great to have your son vacuum the house, mow the lawn, and take advantage of his new license by gassing up the car and buying the weekly groceries. Is he cutting himself off from his peers at the same time? Do you feel as if you and he are on a date when you have meals alone together or go out? Do you listen to him when he starts telling you how to wear your hair, or whom to entertain, or how to spend your money? If so, his involvement with your life may be keeping each of you from reaching out to people outside the family in appropriate ways.

You're relieved that your fourteen-year-old daughter doesn't have a fit when your new man friend spends the night. She seems relaxed with him around and you begin to relax also. Then she hits you with the classic question: "If your boyfriend sleeps over, why can't mine?" In your confusion, you are tempted to give in. *Don't.* Remember, you are a mature adult who has been through a marriage. Sex outside of marriage is vastly different when you're forty from when you're fourteen.

Teenagers and children who are required to take on the responsibilities of a second adult in the family may seem to be adjusting well. However, difficulties can appear later on. The child may have trouble leaving home, for example, when it is an appropriate time to do so. Physical symptoms, substance abuse, eating disorders, and delinquency can also be signs that a teenager feels burdened by adult worries.

Keeping the generation gap alive is one of your jobs as a parent. If you feel you cannot do this without support, look for another adult, not your child, to help you. Not only will your child benefit, but it will be much easier to form a relationship with a new partner if your child has not become your guardian. Your new man or woman friend will appreciate your independence.

THE VISITING MINIFAMILY

While the custodial parent has more of the same familial responsibilities after a divorce, the visiting parent has to adjust to a very different form of parenting. Both parents and children find the role of the visiting parent (usually a father) a mystery.

Do I treat him like an uncle now—someone who remembers my birthday and takes me out to dinner? What do I do with him? [A sixteen-year-old girl referring to her visiting father.]

Does he have the right to visit the kids when he wants or the responsibility to take them every week? I count on that time. If he decides he's not coming, I'm up a creek. Besides, the kids need to see him. [A divorced mother of three children, ages eight, six, and two.]

What do you do with three kids you only see on Sunday afternoons? If you take them to your house, they pick on each other all the time and say they're bored. If I take them out all the time, it costs a fortune and I feel more like a tour director than a father. How do you pack all that fathering into one day a week? [A divorced father of three children, ages fourteen, eleven, and seven.]

Although no one has a definitive solution to the mystery, research with children whose parents are divorced has taught us that regular contact with their fathers is one of the best ways to help children adjust to divorce. Just as the fathers get satisfaction from peeking in at their sleeping children, the children seem to feel reassured knowing that Dad is nearby.

The time and effort you can put into creating a role for yourself as a visiting father pays off in better mental and emotional growth for your children. Moreover, what seems like a nearly insignificant amount of time together (for example, visits limited to Sundays from 10 a.m. to 6 p.m.) becomes very important through constant repetition. Eight or ten years of Sunday visits can add up to a close and important relationship.

Some visiting parents find that the time they spend with their children, though limited, is a major focus of their lives. The father of a three-year-old and a seven-year-old describes his week:

> Sunday is my day with the kids, but I start planning it on Tuesday. I never thought I could miss them so much. Jimmy can hardly talk straight but I miss his smile and the funny way he runs. So I think of what we'll do together, where we'll go. When I do my grocery shopping, I think of them when I buy animal crackers and ice-cream pops, things I would never eat. Then, by Saturday, I'm really missing them a lot. Once I turned down a party invitation because I wanted to get up early Sunday to drive to Springfield to get the kids. Sunday goes by too quickly. After I take them home, I'm exhausted. It takes all day Monday to recover. Tuesday I start gearing up for next week.

This father probably spends more time now thinking specifically about his children and their needs than he did before his separation. It is one way of soothing his own pain and protecting himself from new relationships. He is not likely to meet many women while his energy is focused on his children, and he probably needs time off from adult intimacy to recover from his divorce.

What is unusual about the visiting minifamily is that the members spend more time apart than together. The times when the minifamily is together can bring up the feelings of loss and anger that both parent and children feel when they are separated. Having a cheerful, fun-filled visit, which is what most of us think we should do, is difficult when the underlying feelings are those of pain and sorrow. Sometimes it is best to share these sad feelings with your children.

TRANSITIONS

The visits are also framed by the transition time after the children arrive from their custodial home and the transition time before they leave. Transitions become easier with time, but they are always a fact of divorced life to be reckoned with. Some children need alone time; the first thing they do is to go off by themselves and make the adjustment privately. Others need physical contact, sitting on Dad's lap or wrestling. Still others do best if they can focus on a structured activity, a game of Frisbee or Monopoly, to defuse their intense feelings. Transition rituals continue after a remarriage and become part of the stepfamily's routine as well.

For the child, transition time is often a chance to switch loyalties. One six-year-old boy who left his mother's home on Thursday afternoon, to spend long weekends with his father, would make a present for his mother each weekend. At first, this was a Sunday morning activity in anticipation of the return to Mom. After several months, it became an activity for Thursday evening. He made the present, put it away somewhere safe, and was ready for Dad. Several months later still, the present-making ritual was no longer necessary.

Transitions are hard on parents, too. The visiting mother of a four-year-old described her despair after returning the child to her father's home each Sunday night. "I just fall apart. I cry for hours. I keep thinking this is not right. I still have nightmares about the courtroom in which he [her ex-husband] got her."

Transitions are also difficult for the custodial parent. Seeing the children leave may bring feelings of sadness as well as relief. When they return, they often seem particularly edgy, overtired, and cranky. A common complaint is that the ex-spouse must be doing something terribly wrong during the visitation time because the children come home in such bad shape. This situation is so typical, however, that we must conclude it is a result of the transition itself and not the particular parent's behavior during the visit.

There are ways to make the transition times a little easier. For example:

- Reminding the children of the time they will be going or coming is important. Children are usually calmer when they can anticipate the schedule.

- Bringing a few transitional objects on the visit helps the children to establish a home base wherever they are. A favorite toy, a special blanket or doll are common objects of attachment for little children. Older children may want to bring new records, a piece of sports equipment, or a special article of clothing. Although these objects may not be practical necessities for the visit, they are useful emotionally.

- Sometimes returning the kids several hours before bedtime gives them a chance to adjust to being in their primary home again and helps them settle down before they have to get to bed. Then they are more rested the next morning. Letting your children know you'll miss them—without pressuring them to miss you as much—allows them to have their own feelings.

- Recognizing your child's feelings is a way to give support. Such statements as "It's hard to say good-bye," or "Lots of people feel sad when they have to leave a mommy or daddy for a few days," can help children to accept their feelings as normal and legitimate. The child's tears or crankiness (another way of expressing sadness) may be painful to you and difficult to control, but accepting this part of your child is also part of being a good parent.

One result of the visitation schedule that many parents overlook is the closeness which develops between brothers and sisters. If the children are spending part of their time with each parent, they are the only members of the family who are almost always in the same place at the same time. Although you may want to discourage them from becoming too bossy or too protective of each other, you may also want to praise them for looking after each other as they move back and forth through the month.

CHANGES IN THE PARENTAL ROLE

The scope of parenting also changes in the visiting relationship. For some parents, particularly men who did not have primary child care responsibilities, the range of care is increased. Even fathers who cared for their children frequently before the divorce may feel overwhelmed by total management of the children for a few days. One father found a big difference between playing with the children on Sunday mornings so his wife could sleep a little later and playing with the children on Sunday mornings while his ex-wife slept in another apartment.

I used to enjoy this time. Tommy and I would build with the blocks and make parades of toy trucks. When Benji got fussy and needed to nurse, I would tiptoe into the bedroom and give him to Marianne, who would take him into the bed with her. Now when he fusses, I have to give him a bottle and Tommy gets jealous and climbs all over me. Meantime, no one is fixing my breakfast, no one is there when I need a shower or the phone rings. If I forget to buy Pampers, I have to load the kids in the car and it becomes a major expedition.

Other visiting parents find their roles more limited than before. They miss the little contacts, giving their children help with homework, taking a walk to buy milk, being there when the child gets up with a nightmare, or seeing the delighted face of the child at his birthday party. They feel excluded from the daily decisions.

If you do not have a home you can bring the children to, or if you live at some distance from their home, you may find yourself spending a lot of time together in parks, zoos, movies, and restaurants. Visiting in public places is not conducive to intimacy. You have to pay attention to parking places, prices, and manners. You can't roughhouse as you would at home. You can't even yell at a disobedient child when you feel it is deserved. The children get tired and overstimulated. Sometimes they are tempted by the many items for sale and seem constantly to be asking you to buy them something. You may begin to think of them as greedy and spoiled because you don't see them in a home environment.

Another difficulty is finding activities that are enjoyable for children of different ages. The fifteen-year-old wants to go to a basketball game, and the eight-year-old still likes the zoo. In a nuclear family, each could have a turn to go to the preferred place, but you can't do both on the same Saturday afternoon.

The visiting relationship later becomes part of the stepfamily. Some of these difficulties remain even after a remarriage has taken place. They then become family problems rather than the sole concern of the visiting parent. How the visit has been handled influences the formation of the stepfamily.

Ted's children were used to spending one weekend a month with him in his small apartment. They brought their sleeping bags and camped out in his study or living room, since he didn't have any extra beds. The weekend had its special routines, which included picking out their favorite foods at the grocery store, telling ghost stories after dark, and jumping into their father's bed in the morning.

When Ted and Virginia started living together in Virginia's house, which was more spacious than Ted's apartment, she suggested he bring the boys there for their visit. For the first few months he declined and kept his own place, primarily for the boys' visits. Virginia thought he was holding on to his apartment in case he changed his mind about living with her. She felt very insecure about it.

When Ted finally did move out of his former place and his children began to visit at Virginia's, they all felt uncomfortable. The children had a guest room to themselves, but it was not as much fun as their sleeping bags. They knew they couldn't jump into Virginia's bed in the morning. Virginia, too, felt like an outsider when Ted arrived with two kids and a trunk full of groceries and started cooking without even consulting her. The feelings of exclusion and rejection were caused by the coming together of two minifamilies, Ted's visiting minifamily and the new-couple minifamily. Each minifamily brought its own history and traditions with it.

TEMPTATIONS

The visiting parent has a hard job. You may be tempted to avoid the difficulties and pain of this task by:

1. Not visiting your children. If you don't see your children, you don't have to talk to your former spouse and you don't have to feel the pain of saying good-bye to your children each time. Your life feels less complex, and you can think you are free to start over. But your children probably miss you. They may be in great pain because they cannot see you. They may even blame themselves for pushing you away. Your absence may contribute to problems that will interfere with their growth. Moreover, your pain does not go away. It may be hidden below the surface and remain there for years.

2. Focusing all your energy on your children both when you are with them and when you are not. This course may be natural

for the first few months of separation and is not likely to hurt the children. However, it is also a way to avoid recognizing that the divorce is really happening and facing the separation from your children as well as your wife. Besides, you need some time for yourself.

3. Letting someone else take over the visits for you.

Some men find that their parents are very happy to provide a home base for their visits with their children. These men run into the problem that Stella experienced when she moved back into her parents' home. Grandparents who are providing the space, the food, and the postvisit cleanup operation often want the final word, the hugs, and the kisses. You may begin to feel like your children's brother, being reminded to wash your hands before meals. This is not the model of a parent you want to present to your children.

If you find yourself in a new relationship very soon after your separation, you may discover that the new woman in your life knows more about children than you do. She may either be a mother herself or just have the knack of knowing how to talk to children and what to expect from them. It is easy to let her plan the visits, care for the kids, and leave you free to watch the Sunday afternoon ball game on TV. If you find this happening in your life, don't forget that your children need *you*. They are confused and conflicted about forming an attachment to a new mother figure, but they know they need a father. You may find yourself, at a later date, being resentful and angry of the way this new woman has reorganized *your* family.

Although creating a visiting minifamily is hard work, it pays off later on when you have your children's affection and appreciation for your efforts, and when you can feel proud of yourself for not abandoning the children.

SEX ROLES

We have been describing custodial mothers and visiting fathers because these are the most common arrangements. However, more and more divorcing couples are choosing to have joint legal custody, in which they share nearly equally the child-rearing decisions and responsibilities. Even when couples have a more traditional custody arrangement, the father may be an active participant in the children's day-to-day care. If you are a custodial father or a visiting mother, you have probably recognized that you are not in a unique situation.

Through parenting alone after divorce, you may learn that tasks you thought had to be done by a mother or a father can actually be performed by either parent. Men learn to cook, diaper, and buy clothes for their children. Women fix appliances around the house, mow the lawn, and teach their children to play baseball. Necessity teaches many divorced parents that they are not as limited by their sex as they had thought.

You may feel uncomfortable, nonetheless, when you are the only father at a birthday party for your daughter's three-year-old play-mate and all the mothers are sitting together while the children play. You may wonder what you, as the only mother, are doing at your son's father-son camping trip. Although you feel awkward, you can remind yourself that your child appreciates your participation and that, sooner or later, other parents will find themselves in similar circumstances.

THE PARADOX

The choices you make and the actions you take as a divorced parent have very different implications for the long and short term. In order to keep yourself and your children emotionally healthy, you must form a new minifamily with its own boundary. This adjustment for survival is likely to become an obstacle toward forming a stepfamily later on. Nevertheless, you cannot merely keep your family as it is while waiting for the right partner to come along. The necessities of everyday life in a family with children require that all of you adjust. If you did not adjust, you would certainly not be a fit mate for anyone in the future.

John was an engineer in a high-tech company. His wife of sixteen years planned an elaborate party for him on his fortieth birthday. The next day she did not come home from work. He received a telegram saying that she had to go off by herself and evaluate her life, that she would write to the children, who were fifteen and thirteen. John felt himself go cold inside; he thought his heart was freezing.

He could barely talk to the children, but he was very good at engineering. He planned their daily routines so that the kids worked together on dinners and chores and the house was cared for. He freed up some time in the afternoons to help them with their activities, see their teachers, or shop for groceries. He was very proud of his efficient new organization. His daughter teased him by saying that he must have worked it out on his computer. His friends marveled at how smoothly he seemed to have taken over the primary parenting role.

The first person to find a flaw in the system was Janice, a woman he met just after he turned forty-two. She felt she had to fit in between John's night to cook and his night to take the kids shopping. She invited John and his children to dinner only to be told this was their night to eat out. When she visited, she was treated as a guest. They even turned down her offer to help with the dishes. The children and their father seemed to be in a conspiracy aimed at keeping her outside the center of their family.

John and Janice continued to see each other for several years. After both children had gone away to college, they finally started living together. They were married shortly thereafter.

Although the story ended in a good second marriage for John, he had a hard time moving into the remarriage from the position he had created in the single-parent minifamily. His rigid rules about caring for his household and family had served two functions. The conscious function was to keep up the everyday chores so that the children would experience as little disruption in their routines as possible. The underlying goal was to cover up the deep pain and despair that neither he nor his children could easily acknowledge. To let Janice into the family as a participant in the nurturing tasks of daily life would have been threatening because it might have created a hole in the armor through which those painful feelings could emerge.

His short-term solution worked for his own and his children's adjustment at the time of their abandonment but created problems in the long run. Luckily, the problems were not insoluble. The hard work of living in a stepfamily is often solving the problems created by the previous, very good, solutions.

CHAPTER FOUR

Introducing Children and New Partners

The lights dim and the movie begins. It is the story of a single mother and the double identity she is obliged to assume. We see her in the kitchen of her apartment. She is cooking dinner, talking on the telephone, and making out birthday invitations simultaneously. Two young boys enter. They sit down at the table. She hangs up the phone, puts the invitations aside, and serves dinner. She jokes with her children, tells them about their cleanup jobs, and answers the same riddle wrong seven times. The mothers in the audience notice the stress lines around her eyes, the flyaway hair, her obvious fatigue. But she continues to smile and talk sweetly to her two energetic boys.

SCENE TWO

Is this the same actress? The makeup department has performed marvels. She's seated at a quiet table for two in an elegant restaurant. The waiter is asking her male companion to taste the wine. Our heroine is still smiling, but her smiles have a different meaning. She is alluring and flirtatious. She talks sweetly to her charming host. She dances gracefully. We are more admiring of her than ever.

SCENE TEN

Our single mother is seated on a picnic blanket with her two lively sons. The boys are not actually seated. They are bouncing up and down pretending to be kangaroos. Our heroine is gently chiding them and giving more wrong answers to the same senseless riddles. This time, though, she's dressed and made up like the woman in the restaurant. *Aha*, it's becoming clear. This is the scene in which Mr. Right will be introduced to her sons. She looks at her watch and smiles. He will arrive soon.

We in the audience feel tense. We have seen the heroine trying to control two very active boys. We have heard her describe them to Mr. Right, but we know she underplayed their energy and incessant chatter. We have also seen how attentive she is to Mr. Right. What will the boys think of that? She has described him as an athletic hero who loves popcorn and Michael Jackson. She has not told them that he likes to hold her hand and kiss her. It's not that our heroine has been lying. It's just that she's eager to have the three males in her life like each other. She's been doing a public relations job on either end.

Although her intentions are good, we can see that she faces some really tough problems. Mr. Right has never understood why our single mother always has to be home at the stroke of 1 a.m., the teenage baby-sitter's deadline. Then, too, there's no time for mushiness when Mr. Right is expected to drive the sleepy fourteen-year-old sitter home. The bouncing boys resent Mommy's long phone calls. She laughs more on the phone than she does at their riddles. And they wonder why they have so many baby-sitters. They are beginning to make the connections.

We return our attention to the screen. We have missed the introductions but are in time to catch some choice dialogue:

MR. RIGHT: Darling, what a lovely spot for a picnic.

FIRST SON: Mommy, why did the elephant—

MOTHER: Yes, I'm so glad you could come. The children—

FIRST SON: Why did the elephant sit on—

MR. RIGHT: Remember that cousin of mine I was telling—

SECOND SON: I know, why did the elephant sit on the picnic blanket?

FIRST SON: Mommy, he's teasing me.

MOTHER: Which cousin was that?

FIRST SON: Mommy, you're not paying attention.

The conversation quickly goes downhill when the boys start wrestling and tip over the picnic basket. We silently cringe as our heroine, for the first time, is not in control of it all.

If you are a single parent who has tried introducing the children to a new Mr. or Ms. Right, you may consider this film a rerun. The movie picnic may have turned out to be delightful, but in real life it could have been a dud. Your parent-child minifamily and your new-couple minifamily develop in different times and different ways. Your children have one set of expectations for you, your lover has another. You have different standards for yourself in each situation. Bringing the two systems together, even for an afternoon, is not a simple undertaking.

THE DATING PHASE

Even a relationship that is kept secret can affect the children by changing your behavior as their parent. Children are very sensitive to their parents' moods and feelings. Your children have seen you and your former spouse change because of the divorce. These changes are unsettling. Very young children may not even know whether the new behavior means you are happy, sad, or angry. They may assume that the change in you is caused by something that they did, like making the TV too loud. An older school-aged child may ask you what's happening. If you don't give a reasonable reply, the child may suspect some awful secret that you cannot reveal. An adolescent is apt to guess that you have met someone special and may ask more questions than you would like to answer.

Many parents try to keep their dating lives apart from their children. Nonetheless, falling in love is an intense and tumultuous experience. As a divorced parent in a new relationship, you may be tired, silly, distracted, grouchy, or elated. You get as worked up over an expected phone call as an adolescent. You may be aware of what causes your moodiness, but you are not likely to say to your child, "I'm yelling at you for spilling that milk because Ed hasn't called in three days." Nor do you say, "I don't care if you don't do your practicing tonight because I'm in love."

Your Time Conflict

As your adult relationship develops, you are bound to have times when you cannot be both with your new friend and your children. If you do not want your New Person to meet the children right away, or if you want some privacy, you are going to have to make choices about how you spend your time. You may be upset when you cannot be in two places at once. The children will probably be angry and hurt when you don't choose them.

If your children are young, you may find yourself leaving them with baby-sitters more often. Cozy Saturday evenings watching old movies together give way to baby-sitters and dates. In your excitement about the new relationship, you are less likely than your children to miss those intimate moments. When your former husband is coming to pick up the children and you are expecting your new friend to arrive half an hour later, you may find yourself thinking about the afternoon you'll spend with him rather than saying good-bye to your children. They notice the difference.

As a visiting parent, your absence from home is noticed by your children when they cannot reach you by phone. They ask you to take them for dinner and, for the first time in a year and half, you turn them down. They may feel hurt and rejected.

Your feelings about the time you spend with your children are likely to change when you become involved with someone new. Ron was a visiting father who had been very enthusiastic about entertaining his children on their visits, as much to fill up his own empty spot as to satisfy them. When he started dating a new woman, he put his energy into taking her out. During the children's visits, he felt like staying home and relaxing. His six-year old was content to play with toy cars in the dining room and go on errands with Ron. The older children, however, were disappointed and bored. Their visits had lost their liveliness and excitement.

Kathy became more permissive with her children after her husband left. She did not have the emotional stamina to make sure they got all their chores done, and she certainly couldn't keep the house in tip-top shape without their help. When she met a new man whom she really liked, she didn't want him to think she lived in a pigpen. She started having what her children called "cleaning fits" before his visits. Since he often came while the children were with their father, the cleaning fits frequently occurred while the children were packing their things for a weekend visit. The children felt resentful that their mother was not helping them and that she suddenly seemed so preoccupied with neatness and cleanliness. For the first time in two years, her seven-year-old cried when it was time to leave for the weekend and didn't want to go with her father.

This was not the only change Kathy's children had to face—even before they met Mr. Wonderful. She also realized that her children had become fresh and ill-mannered. She began a good-manners campaign and tried to reestablish the habit of obedience. The children knew she was doing this so they would make a good impression on someone. They became rebellious and uncooperative.

Children's Initial Reactions

Living in a minifamily with a dating parent is a bit like living in a family with an adolescent. The new attachment, while healthy and exciting for the parent, seems like a threat to the status quo and to the attachment between parent and children. Although the children may be able to benefit considerably from a new relationship that flourishes and grows to include them, they rarely welcome it with outstretched arms.

If you are a custodial parent and your former spouse is entering a new relationship, your relationship with your children may also be affected by it. For example:

- Your children complain to you that Dad doesn't take them to their favorite pizza place because "she" is allergic to pizza.

- Your children want to stay with you instead of visiting because "she" will be there.

- Your children can't wait for their visit because "she" will be there.

- You and your children share your misery about "her" existence.

- You hate your children because they like "her" and you don't.

If you are a visiting parent and your former spouse is dating someone new, your relationship with your children may be affected by it. For example:

- Your children don't want to visit you because they want to be sure "he" doesn't touch their home computer.
- Your children don't want to visit you because they want to stay home and spy on their mother and "him."
- Your children don't want to go home after their visits because they don't want to see "him" or his kids.
- You laugh at your children's imitations of "him" and feel closer to them because you all dislike this guy.
- You are furious at your children for liking "him" and make them wash the floor when they visit you.

Sometimes the children do not see why you need a new adult partner. After all, you have them. One benefit of the divorce, as they see it, is the chance to have *you* all to themselves. Remember, they barely recognize your emotional existence as a person outside of the parental role. If they do understand your desire for adult companionship, they're likely to come up with an easy solution: Get back together with your ex-spouse.

This difference in attitude between you and the children may upset the closeness and comfort you have been working toward. To emphasize your minifamily solidarity, you've been focusing on things you and the children have in common: a fondness for Chinese restaurants, the fun of baseball games.

Now you are faced with an issue on which disagreement is built in, based on the difference in your ages and your needs as individuals. Your children may consider your interest in dating a serious betrayal of the minifamily. You may be hurt by their negative comments. There is no way around it. You are going to have to cope with the children's responses to dating, to new people in your life, and to remarriage, and these responses won't necessarily be the same as yours.

Your children are not doing this on purpose to wreck your life; they are doing it on purpose to maintain a status quo to which they have adjusted. You are initiating more changes, and they are finding it difficult to keep up with you.

Children's Conflicts About the New Person

A new adult member of the family is not a part of your child's agenda. The child is a step or two behind you in accepting the changes brought about by the divorce. When you have finally let go and are ready to enrich your life, your child may still be letting go of the former family. In addition, the presence of a new adult creates a complex loyalty conflict for the child.

Young children, we recall, see relationships as a function of physical proximity. They are likely to interpret the presence of a New Person at the dinner table, in the car, or going out with you as a replacement for the parent who is no longer there. Sitting in Daddy's chair literally means taking Daddy's place. Children's loyalty to the other parent dictates that they not allow a New Person to take over that role. You try to explain that "Mommy is still your mommy and Daddy is still your daddy," but the children may find it hard to understand this concept. They have no intellectual framework in which to place this new idea. Even children whose intellectual and cognitive skills are advanced in other areas—such as schoolwork, ability to understand computer languages, or proficiency at dramatic games—can have a hard time understanding these family changes.

Children often seem to favor the parent who is absent or who seems (from a child's point of view) to be getting the raw end of the deal. If your six-year-old becomes unhappy when you take him out to dinner with your new woman friend, he may be thinking that his mother would like to be going out to dinner. Here you are lavishing attention on someone new while his mother is home all alone. He is not likely to think about the fact that actually she may be out with someone else. The young child imagines that the parent is exactly where he left her. One little girl accompanied her father to the airport when he left for an extended trip. Several days later someone asked her where her daddy was. She replied, "He's in that big airplane."

Your children may also feel that because you like someone new, you want and expect them to like the New Person also. (And let's face it, usually you do.) This may seem like an order they cannot obey, and yet they have no way of telling you. Differences of opinion can seem threatening to the child's security in the minifamily.

Adolescents

Somewhere between the ages of twelve and fifteen the child begins to see each parent as a separate adult with a unique personality that is fairly stable over time. Mom-and-Dad, even in a nuclear family, become Mother and Father, two separate people who have differences. In fact, teenagers often test this new concept by playing the two parents off against each other when they are denied something by one of them.

The adolescent is also beginning to become interested in members of the opposite sex and can understand your desire to have a new partner. In fact, the dating stage is often one of competition between adolescent and parent. Statements such as these are not uncommon:

"It's not fair. My mom goes out more than I do."

"She's borrowing my blouses to go on her dates."

"I hate staying home alone when my son is out with his girlfriend."

"Every time the phone rings, we both run to answer it."

Despite the adolescent's own experience, he or she may not be as sympathetic to your desire to meet new people as you would like. After all, adolescents also have to overcome the pain of divorce. Moreover, they are preparing to be the ones to go out into the world, meet new people, and have you there as a steady home base when they want to come back. How can they zigzag in and out of the family if you are zagging out at the time that they want to be zigging in? You and the adolescent may both have a sense of abandonment and a feeling that your minifamily is falling apart.

TIME FOR INTRODUCTIONS

We have seen that the mere fact that you, a divorced parent, are dating someone new—someone your children may not have even met—disrupts your minifamily. Bringing the children together with the person who is lighting up your life is even trickier. This is when you may start feeling as if you are the rope in a game of tug-of-war.

The picnic in our make-believe movie is an example of what happens when two minifamilies are brought together for the first time. Each minifamily expects the day to proceed the way it usually does, but these expectations may be vastly different. You, the one person who is a member of both minifamilies, may see the problem of dual expectations but feel powerless to solve it. How can you answer riddles endlessly and carry on an adult conversation at the same time? How can you look glamorous and pick up a muddy toddler? How can you cook a gourmet dinner and spend the afternoon playing basketball?

When you initially bring together your children and your new man or woman friend, your children may be disturbed by small details that would have seemed unimportant to you:

- Kathy's children were stunned when Mr. Right finally came to dinner because, instead of asking like a guest for more butter, he went to the refrigerator and helped himself. They wanted to show him their rooms and were disappointed that he already knew who slept where.

- David was surprised when the man coming to dinner brought him a toy car. "I guess you didn't know my birthday is in March," he said diplomatically. Later, he asked his mother, "Who is he to me? Why did he give me a birthday present?"

- Tricia was furious when she and her father went to pick up his new friend. The woman wanted Tricia to give up her place in the front seat next to her dad.

- Jonathan was shocked when his former nursery school teacher spent the afternoon with him and his dad and kissed his father good-bye. He was beyond thinking that teachers sleep under their desks at night, but he thought this teacher had disappeared when he grew too old to attend nursery school.

Older children criticize the new guest in other ways: He talks too loud. He thinks you're his servant. She has no taste. He tells bad jokes. Her hair isn't cut right. She has a phony accent. She treats us like little kids.

Suppose Mr. or Ms. Right also has children. Now three minifamilies are involved. Your children are jealous when you pay attention to the other children. Those kids tease your children. Your partner is jealous when his children smile at you. If you both have young children, you can sometimes pull off a nice outing. Two three-year-olds can be put side by side in a sandbox to enjoy themselves. A fourteen-year-old and a ten-year-old who have just met cannot be sent out to the yard to play.

PLANNING A STRATEGY

You have a disastrous introductory meeting. You and your new woman friend, Diane, take all the children to a movie. What could be simpler? All they have to do is sit and watch the screen. You discover, however, that her kids have to use the bathroom every half hour. Your two insist on sitting like bodyguards on either side of you, holding your hands. You don't even have a finger free to tap Diane on the shoulder. After the movie you suggest buying a pizza, but the children can't agree on what kind to get. By the end of the day, you are ready to trade places with the Secretary General of the United Nations. You wonder if you've wrecked what looked like a promising relationship or, rather, if your kids have wrecked it for you.

This situation is going to require more planning than you had anticipated. The hardest part of planning your strategy is to define the problem in clear and simple terms. Making people like each other, for example, is not a goal you can attain, so you cross out "How to get Diane's children to like me." This is too vague anyway. You also cross out "Bribing my children to like Diane's children and Diane."

"How to get all the children to leave us alone so I can enjoy Diane's company" is better, but it's still very broad. Finally, you settle on a long-term goal that can be broken down into smaller steps: "Helping my minifamily and Diane's minifamily get together."

1. I should meet Diane's kids at home where they feel secure.
2. Diane should meet my children at home where they are calmer.
3. The grown-ups should make the decisions.
4. Diane and I should not stop seeing each other alone; including the children will take time and effort.
5. We should all get together at a later date.
6. We should get together after the kids have had a chance to spend some time with their own parent.

You also select a more specific goal for your children that will help achieve the larger goal: "Preparing my children to be with Diane and me." You decide on a subgoal: "Teaching my children to allow me to converse with grown-ups in their presence without frequent interruptions."

1. Do not allow them to interrupt each other.
2. Make sure I listen to them when they have something to say and have been waiting.
3. Don't interrupt them.
4. Don't allow them to interrupt phone conversations.
5. Praise them for waiting.

This kind of goal setting will help you to be a better parent all the time, not only with Diane. Moreover, your insistence on good manners will not depend on Diane's presence, so the children will not resent her for it.

A project such as getting together with Diane and her children, and expecting the children to allow the adults some time to talk, usually requires work within each minifamily. Children meet new people most easily when they feel secure and feel they have been getting enough attention from you. When you remember their needs and make sure they are not hungry, tired, or worried, they are likely to be friendly and calm. Taking your children to a 9 o'clock dinner in a fancy restaurant may seem like a treat to you and an ordeal to them.

As part of your strategy, you could plan for Diane and your children to meet again. This time you want things to go more smoothly. You think the children will be better behaved and appear more civilized if they have already spent some of their visiting time with you. You realize that if Diane comes to your house for Sunday brunch without her kids (who visit their father on Sundays), your children will be able to amuse themselves while you and Diane chat over a second cup of coffee. You also plan something special for them, a dessert they like, enjoyable jobs to do, or permission to watch a favorite TV show.

In trying this strategy, you may discover a fortunate paradox. The more you make an effort to include your children and anticipate their needs, the more they will give you the space you want from them. When they know they are cared for, they become less clingy.

When planning strategies on your own, you need to consider the ages of your children. Teenagers are not as willing as younger children to be included in adult-planned outings, but they will often agree to invite your New Person to an activity they enjoy. If you have children who need naps and snacks, your best bet is to make provisions for these needs. Otherwise, you will end up with very cranky children and disappointed adults. You also need to think about the ways you usually do things. Plan a strategy that you can carry off. Don't invite Diane and her children to a ballet if you hate classical music. Don't make a trip to the zoo if your four-year-old gets tired easily and has to be carried.

Strategy Checklist

1. Are my goals clear?
2. Does this strategy make sense for me, as I am?
3. Do I have several smaller steps leading up to a larger goal?
4. Have I considered the other people's ages and tastes?
5. Should I talk this over with my new friend and/or my children before I implement my plan or any part of it?

If your strategy doesn't work, it is helpful to review what you thought you were trying to accomplish and how and why you did not succeed, just as you would in a business venture. Did you forget how long the drive is to that special amusement park? Did you go ahead with a plan even though your youngest child looked a little pale and seemed to be coming down with something? Did

you leave your sense of humor at home because you were so determined to do this right? Did you stick to your plans rigidly even
when it was clear that they were not working?

You may think you're expending too much effort over just having your friend come to dinner at your house when your children
are there. However, taking an exercise like this seriously a few
times can benefit you and your family in many ways. When you get
used to thinking about people's needs (including your own) and
anticipating how you will provide for them, you may find that:

- You pay more attention to things as they are happening.
  You have increased your consciousness of the needs and
  responses of the people in your family.
- You are more sensitive to people at work.
- When things go well, you feel a sense of accomplishment
  and pride.
- You have better times alone with your children as well as
  when you bring them together with other people.
- When events do not turn out the way you would like them
  to, you can look for the reasons rather than feeling victim-
  ized or inadequate.

THE ROLE OF THE FUTURE
STEPPARENT

Being a stepparent is hard. Becoming a stepparent is even harder.
And spending time with a divorced parent and his or her children
may be harder still. You are confined to a small safety zone, one
that is not clearly demarcated in any way. If you come on too strong
with the children, they become suspicious and aloof. If you are not
friendly to them at all, you know their parent is disappointed in
you.

You have your own inclinations to care for the children, to discipline them, or to ignore them. However, you often find yourself
questioning your gut reactions and thinking about what is expected
of you in your new role. What is your role anyway? Are you an
almost-stepparent? Can you be sure of that?

At the beginning of your relationship with your new friend and his or her children, you are clearly an outsider because you are not a member of the parent-child minifamily. Your membership in the couple minifamily gives you certain rights with your friend, but these do not necessarily carry over to the children. Your best bet is to remain on the outside and gently work your way in.

You can be a good partner by helping the divorced parent to be a better parent. Whether or not the children like you is immaterial at this stage. Even if they barely acknowledge your existence (which, by the way, is not ususual), you can be helpful to your friend and to the parent-child minifamily by offering feedback on your partner's behavior as a parent, by sharing your observations of the children, and by gently making suggestions based on your own experience. If you think your woman friend's children need more discipline, for example, and you have only met them three times, your best bet is to praise and support your friend when she sets limits rather than stepping in actively. Disciplining the children will earn you a good deal of resentment, whereas supporting your friend may gain you appreciation.

If you are able to add enjoyment and optimism to your partner's life, you are also contributing to the entire minifamily. You may be the one with enough energy left at the end of the day for telling funny stories or suggesting a trip to the ice-cream parlor. The love that you and your friend share may help your friend to be more patient and loving with the children.

You may recall that a single parent is often burdened by having sole responsibility for the children. Unfortunately, sometimes you become the backup for such chores as washing the dishes while the parent gets the children ready for bed, or running errands that can't be done with the children along. You may not get the rewarding tasks, like good-night stories or holding a child on your lap in the movies. You are often stuck with the dishes so that your partner and you can spend some time together after the child goes to bed. If you leave the dishes, you and your friend will have to wait even longer before concentrating on each other.

Jealousy

Many adults who are dating someone with children are embarrassed to admit that they are sometimes jealous of the children. You may find yourself envying your friend's closeness with the children, resenting their importance in his or her life, and wanting more attention for yourself. After all, the two of you are in love. What happened to the old expression, "I only have eyes for you"? Getting used to sharing the attention of your mate with children can be difficult. If you find yourself having these feelings, don't automatically assume you are becoming a wicked stepparent.

Rejection

Feelings of rejection are another frequent problem for people in your position. Adults who are not parents themselves seem particularly vulnerable to becoming very attached to a child, working hard to be friendly and giving to the child, and finding themselves out in the cold when their overtures are not reciprocated. If you are feeling rejected by your friend's child, stop worrying about what is wrong with you. Children do not read some obscure corner of your mind in which you are really a wicked person. They are probably so involved with their own development and feelings that they cannot cope with you.

How to Proceed

You will discover later on that becoming close to stepchildren is a three-stage process which can take from two to five years. At this point, you are not even in stage one. The best advice is:

- *Go slowly.* The children are probably still adjusting to the divorce or to the possibility that their parent likes another adult.
- *Focus your attention on the adult.* A man can have the cutest children and still not be your one and only. If the new relationship does not work out, you and the children are better off if you have not become too attached to each other.
- *Protect yourself from feeling rejected by a child.* You may not be aware of how much hurt you can feel if you start to love a

child and sense that your love is not returned. Your hurt can later turn into resentment. In the beginning it is best to keep both your positive and negative feelings under control.

- *Don't go overboard*—in giving children presents, planning special activities, or saying how much you love them. Children and their parents are often suspicious of too much too soon, regardless of how genuine your feelings are.
- *Never try to take the other parent's place.* Children are always loyal to both of their parents. Often children who are warming up to you suddenly feel disloyal to their other parent and pull back very quickly. The less you appear to threaten that other parent's place, and the more you can show that you respect their attachment to the other parent, the better chance you have of forming a good relationship in the future.

Remember also the following don'ts:

- Don't cut a child's hair without explicit permission from the custodial parent.
- Don't be affectionate to a child in a way that anyone, the child or either of the parents, could interpret as having sexual overtones. If you feel you cannot trust yourself to refrain from approaching a stepchild sexually, you should never stay alone with that child, and you should seek professional counseling.
- Don't spank the children or discipline them harshly or physically.
- Don't criticize their absent parent when the children are present.

If your adult relationship does not work out, you and the children will not be too hurt by the additional separation. If the relationship does work out well for you and your partner, you will have plenty of time to form a relationship with your stepchildren.

CHAPTER FIVE

Stage One: Acceptance

A nuclear family begins with two members, a man and a woman. Their children automatically become family members. The family history is written around the birth of the children and their growth as they reach important milestones.

A stepfamily begins with two adults and any number of children who are the offspring of the husband or the wife. The family history is woven around getting to know each other, learning to accept and care for family members who are not full blood relatives, who have had very different experiences before the stepfamily began, and who are not eager to be living together.

A family is built through the efforts of you and your spouse as you help each other and your children to function as a whole. The wedding and the legal bonds between you as a new couple are not enough.

The nuclear family is like a home that begins as a small cabin. A bedroom is added to one side when the first child is born. A second-floor bedroom is constructed a few years later. When the children reach their teens, the basement is finished. The house becomes bigger as its original center is extended in different directions.

The stepfamily is more like a home that begins as a three-family house with a strong lock on each of the apartments. The kitchen of one apartment is made larger and the living room becomes a family room for all. A strong lock is installed on the street door so the occupants can feel safe leaving the apartment doors unlocked and moving back and forth between them. One large mailbox replaces the three smaller ones. The back stairs are fixed to provide easy access between the floors. The children hook up an intercom system between their bedrooms. The apartment building has slowly become a unified dwelling place for one family. It may not look just like the single-family house down the street; its history of change and development can be seen where walls have been removed or added. Regardless of these differences, the house does a good job of providing shelter and warmth for its inhabitants.

The goal of your stepfamily is unification, becoming one functional family. The definition of "unify" is "to form into a single unit or a harmonious whole." You want your stepfamily, with all its assorted members, to learn to live together in harmony. Building a stepfamily means learning to act as one family.

Unification is a process that takes from two to four years from the time you all move into the same house. As much as you might like to speed up the process, you will discover that this is nearly impossible. You cannot rush the stepfamily's development; there are too many changes taking place at once. You and your spouse are getting used to being married again. Your children are learning to live with a stepfather, and his children with a stepmother. At the same time, your children are adjusting to a new school, and his children are learning to share their house, yard, and school with yours. His children are working out a new relationship with their mother, who has moved to another state. You and your children are coping with your father's stroke. To make matters more complex, you have learned that you will be laid off in a year and your husband has been offered a promotion that will bring a much-needed raise but will involve longer work hours.

This pile-up of life changes is not unusual in a stepfamily, since each minifamily itself is undergoing changes. You cannot put all your energy into building the stepfamily because your minifamily and your family of origin (the family you were born into) also need help from you. You must balance the needs of the minifamilies and the needs of the stepfamily. If your minifamily is neglected, you and your children may feel that your special relationship has been sacrificed to the stepfamily, and you can all become angry and resentful. If you and your spouse each focus all your attention on your own minifamilies, the stepfamily will never work well and your second marriage may end in divorce.

Stepfamily unification takes place in three major stages: acceptance, authority, and affection. Each stage is necessary for the final goal of a well-functioning family to be realized. The stages may overlap, and the amount of time required for any one stage varies considerably among families. This chapter describes the acceptance stage.

MEMBERSHIP

You become a member of a nuclear family through birth, marriage, or adoption. Family members live in the same house, share the same extended family, are brought up with the same values, celebrate the same holidays, and develop a set of family jokes, expectations, rituals, and patterns of behavior. You take for granted the ways in which members of your family display their membership badges.

You become a member of a stepfamily by getting married for the second time, marrying someone who has been married before, or being the child of someone who remarries. A child is a member of the stepfamily whether the remarried parent's home becomes the primary home or a place to visit. The adults go through a marriage ceremony to mark their commitment to each other, but for the children there is no formal sign of having entered a stepfamily.

When your stepfamily is first formed, there are few signs that the stepfamily members are related. You and your children probably look more alike than you and your partner's children. If the physical differences in size, complexion, or hair are very noticeable, it is easy to divide the stepfamily into his and hers. The members of your stepfamily do not share the same last name. The two parent-child minifamilies are likely to have different kinds of jokes, different standards of neatness, different holiday traditions, and different table manners.

These differences often seem trivial when you are first introduced. You can tolerate a child who eats dinner with you once in a while and chews with his mouth open. But when you realize that your stepson, who is going to be eating hundreds of meals with you each year, chews with his mouth open, you understand how difficult it will be to accept him as part of your family.

A FAMILY OF FAMILIES

If you have never been married, or are divorced and have no children from your previous marriage, your partner's role in another minifamily may be confusing and strange. Accepting her place in the parent-child minifamily means accepting her past marriage, allowing her the time and space to care for her children even when being a good mother to them conflicts with being a good wife to you. You have to recognize that these little children have been loved by your wife longer than you and will sometimes come first in her priorities. Accepting your wife's role in that minifamily means that your family is not going to be just like the nuclear family you grew up in or just like the family next door. This is hard.

Her children are also finding it hard to accept the special relationship you have with their mother. When your wife introduced you to them a year ago as her friend, they thought you'd be stopping by to play tennis or Monopoly. They didn't expect you to move in, insist that they say please and thank you, and use up that extra space in their mom's bed. They don't want to accept your importance to their mother because that means giving up the idea of bringing their father back in, recognizing the fact that you and their mother have secrets from them, and realizing that you are going to be around for a long time. Your minifamily threatens them.

Denial of the past and rejection of your stepchildren and your partner's former spouse are ways of opposing acceptance. You may fantasize that your partner's former marriage never took place. You often wish it had not. When you are reminded by her children's mere existence that your fantasy is only that, you may reject the children in an attempt to deny the reality of the past. You may find them rejecting you for the same reasons. While you and your family are in the acceptance stage of your stepfamily, you will encounter denial and rejection many times.

ACCEPTING DIFFERENCES

We saw earlier how the parent-child minifamilies try to focus on the similarities among their members to promote solidarity. People usually assume that others who are similar to them will like them and others who are different will not. The differences among the minifamilies are most often interpreted as reasons for distrust and fear rather than opportunities for learning about diversity. Therefore, differences which, in themselves, have no meaning take on a negative connotation for remarried couples or their children.

Being suspicious or critical of others who are different probably reflects your own fear of being rejected, criticized, or ridiculed. You have been through a divorce and/or the difficulties of being a single person. You want to spare yourself the risk of being rejected by others, especially by the children of the person you love. You hope they will look, act, and speak just the way you and your children do.

The prior history of the minifamily, or the previous nuclear family, is one that creates differences among the minifamilies. One stepmother described the children in her stepfamily thus:

We were married in 1968. My kids were thirteen and fifteen; his were sixteen and seventeen. We had been living in a small town in Indiana; my first husband was a military man. His [second husband's] boys lived with their mother in New York City. They had hair down to their shoulders and went on peace marches on the weekends. My son had a crewcut and collected stamps.

Despite these differences in lifestyle, the parents were able to accept both sets of children. After some initial shyness and mistrust, the four teenagers learned to speak each other's languages.

In another stepfamily, the wife had spent a year in Mexico with her first husband and her children. She learned to cook many spicy Mexican dishes that she and her children enjoyed. She served them frequently. Her second husband tolerated the Mexican cooking, but his children refused to try it and would make themselves sandwiches to eat instead. The stepmother felt rejected because they did not seem to be giving the Mexican food a chance. The children thought she was purposely cooking food they did not like and felt hurt and rejected by her. This difference in taste, which could have led to sharing and experimenting, became a focal point of competition and mistrust because both the stepchildren and stepmother gave it so much meaning and because the father did not know how to help them talk to each other.

Learning About Minifamily History

Learning about other people's personal and family history is part of becoming closer. Couples spend many hours sharing their past experiences and telling each other their life stories.

In a nuclear family, children and parents share their parental history by telling stories, visiting grandparents and other relatives, and looking at old pictures. In the stepfamily, this kind of sharing is more difficult. Your parents may not be open to a visit from all of you. Your children are reluctant to share the special stories their grandparents tell them. You may not feel comfortable telling your stepchildren the funny and embarrassing stories about your childhood that you have told your own children.

How much do you share the experiences of your first marriage with your new spouse and with the children? You may not like hearing how your husband had to rescue his first wife from a duck pond on their honeymoon. It reminds you of the fact that he married her in the first place. He may not enjoy hearing how your first husband taught you to play the piano, even though playing the piano is something you love to share with all the children.

Listening to the other minifamily's history, which does not include you, can also make you feel excluded. As one stepmother said, "I felt so out of place when Mack would tell Jeanie stories about when she was a baby. Why wasn't I there, too? Why did he insist on talking about times that did not include me and did include Sharon [his ex-wife]?"

If the mother and children had talked more freely about their funny experiences in Mexico before they learned to eat the food that was prepared for them there, the stepchildren might have become more adventurous about tasting the food, but both the mother and children avoided talking about experiences that had occurred in the first marriage.

History also influences our interpretation of present events. Angela divorced her first husband because he beat her and the children. She was horrified when her new husband spanked her son. Her new husband, who was brought up in a household where spankings were given fairly and forgiveness followed quickly, did not understand why she considered this an inappropriate form of discipline. She saw his action as a repeat of her first marriage; he heard her objections as a way of keeping him out of the family.

Expressions of Acceptance

Your assumptions about who is a member of your stepfamily (whom you accept as a family member) may come out in actions you barely thing about:

- Whose names are on the mailbox in your house? The adults? The stepchildren with custody? The stepchildren who visit?
- If one child in the family is having a birthday party, do you try to include the children from the other minifamily?
- Do vacation plans include all, some, or none of the children?
- Do you give all the children about the same number of presents for Christmas, or do you take into account what they are likely to receive from the other parents or grandparents?
- Who does chores, and what are they?

One mother-stepmother hurt her husband's feeling when she took her children—but not his children—for haircuts the day before the school pictures were scheduled. She knew how she wanted her children to look in the photos, but she didn't think it would be right to get her stepchildren's hair cut without permission. Her husband thought she was acting as if his children's pictures were unimportant. He thought she should know that he wanted them to be neat in their pictures.

Personal Differences

If you were a parent before you became a stepparent, you already know that your powers to change your children are limited. Although psychologists used to consider parents the most important influence on a child's personality, they now believe, based on studies of young children and infants, that each child has certain inborn tendencies called "temperament." Your influence as a parent is certainly important, but it is limited by the raw materials with which you have to work.

Children can naturally be active, noisy, neat, competent, social, or pensive. Some children are born shy. As helpful as you can be in giving your children experiences that will boost their confidence or teach them to be friendly to others, a basic shyness is rarely changed. What you do as a parent is help each child cope with his or her makeup.

The family environment also shapes the way in which the child expresses or inhibits his or her traits. Frequent loud arguments within the family, for example, may increase a timid child's fears or make him more immune to argument and criticism. An active child in an active family will appear normal, healthy, and energetic. An active child in a quiet family may be considered hyperactive, aggressive, and restless.

As a parent, you observe the gradual development of your children's personalities. As a stepparent, you see them at a fixed point in time. You cannot determine whether a particular trait is a result of the child's inherent nature, experience in the former nuclear family, experience during the divorce process, or reaction to the new stepfamily. Even a trained psychologist, after doing testing and diagnosis, might not be able to determine the cause of a particular problem or behavior.

To accept a stepchild is not to assume you will change that child later on. Accepting a stepchild is more than acting politely or nicely toward the child. To accept a stepchild is more than merely saying you have accepted him or telling yourself that you must accept her. Acceptance requires time and tolerance.

Suppose that, shortly after your remarriage, you discover that your nine-year-old stepson is afraid to sleep without a night-light. The cause could be:

1. He has always been fearful of the dark.
2. As a young child, he had nightmares. The dark brings up the old fears.
3. He became fearful when his father moved out, and he imagined he had to protect his mother.
4. He became a light sleeper when he realized that you were sleeping in the same bed as his mother and his curiosity about your sex life was aroused.
5. Many nine-year-olds are fearful, and this is a normal phase.

Your initial reaction may be to throw away the night-light and insist that any boy in your family is going to overcome his fears immediately. You will probably meet some resistance from the boy and his mother if you do that.

Your second response might be to accuse his father of being a sissy who has set a poor example for your stepson. You want to show him how tough a man can be. If you pressure him to follow your example, he will probably take it as a criticism of his biological father and you won't get much cooperation.

Finally, you discuss the issue with your wife, who tells you about an attempted burglary that occurred shortly after her divorce. She dates your stepson's fears of the dark to that incident. Together you work out a plan to talk about household protection so that he will feel more secure at night.

Accepting your stepson means accepting for now that he is afraid of the dark and accepting the history that created the fear. Only then can you think about a strategy for change. Stepparents often blame children's negative behavior on the former wife or husband. You are sure your stepdaughter would make her bed at your house if her mother had taught her to do it at her home. You know that your stepson could get better grades if his mother enforced a strict bedtime for him.

You may or may not be right. Even if you are correct, trying to place responsibility for the child's behavior on factors outside of your home makes the problem more complex. First of all, you remind yourself of the former spouse, a person whose existence you would probably rather forget. Second, you create a problem over which you have no control. You are powerless in the former spouse's life. Third, you may be avoiding finding out how much your spouse contributes to the child's behavior and facing some differences between the two of you. Fourth, you postpone working out a practical solution to living with the child in your household. You can learn to see the child as a separate person, not as a constant reminder and representative of the former spouse. You *do* have the power to accept the child and, to the very best of your ability, keep the other parent on the outside of your stepfamily boundary.

Taking a Look at Yourself.

Accepting others who push your buttons also means accepting yourself. Here is an exercise that you can try if you are a member of a stepfamily or even an interested bystander. Think of someone, either a stepfamily member or a close friend or associate, whose behavior you find irksome. Think of a trait that is not a major character flaw (as are extreme selfishness and pathological lying) but that drives you up a wall: talking too loud on the telephone, throwing dirty socks on the floor, or not being able to wake up in the morning. When you have a trait in mind, ask yourself these questions:

1. Is this something that I do myself and am not pleased about?
2. When the person does this, do I feel either guilty or inadequate?
3. Does this remind me of someone in my past?

EXAMPLES

Martin's stepdaughter would make plans with more than one friend for a particular day or evening and would then complain that she felt too pressured by her friends to be with them. When she asked her mother and Martin for advice, he found himself becoming very critical of her behavior. When Martin tried this exercise he realized that he, too, often made more commitments than he could keep and felt very pressured by those to whom he had made promises.

Marion would frequently come home from work to find milk, butter, jam, or other snack ingredients on the kitchen counter. She was angry with both her children and her stepchildren for leaving out foods that could spoil. She accused them of wasting foo' cause they were careless and lazy. When she did the ' realized that she felt guilty that she could not h apron and serving them homemade, d ' when they arrived home from sch guilty feelings about working, she \ dren when they forgot to put away th longer a reflection of her ability to mc

Joan's stepson habitually exaggerate events. The shower on the way home fr downpour. The spaghetti sauce at the ne\ in the entire state. His stories were often ve.

would cringe and clam up when he told them. She secretly accused him of lying. When she did the exercise, she found that his behavior reminded her of her older sister. As a child and adolescent, this sister had always stolen the spotlight by telling uproarious stories. Joan had felt angry, jealous, and helpless.

This exercise can make you focus on the reasons for your reactions to the behaviors you cannot accept. You may discover that knowing and accepting yourself will help you to be less upset by the other people around you.

FAMILY IMAGERY

Ideas are very powerful. Your idea of the perfect family is the standard against which you measure the family you do have. Part of your resistance to accepting your stepfamily is your reaction to being in a family that does not look like or act like your personal image of a family. It is most likely that your imaginary family has no stepchildren. Your imaginary family is quiet and polite. In your imaginary family, the children are happy to visit with their grandparents. Accepting the stepfamily you have means putting that imaginary family away in the attic where it belongs and getting to know the people who are around you.

If you have already been through one marriage, you probably know that most families do not live up to our personal idealistic standards or the picture of family life presented by TV commercials and children's books. If you have never been married before, your image of marriage may be based on fantasies, fairy tales, and Hollywood. Unrealistic standards can become our prison bars. Giving them up frees us to be ourselves and to accept the members of our families as they are.

BOUNDARIES

ond husband or wife, you may feel like an outsider in your
ly. You have a piece of paper that says you are legally
e U.S. census lists you as an official resident of this
heckbook demonstrates that you have been paying

your share of the rent. The mailman delivers mail for you as well as for the other family members. You receive phone calls from friends who recognize that this is your new home.

Why, then, is it so hard to believe that you belong here? Why do you feel like an outsider in your own home? The answer can be summed up simply: *minifamily boundaries.*

Just imagine, for the moment, that the United States had a very weak federal government and very strong state governments. Even though you were officially a citizen of both the United States and Pennsylvania, your credentials had to be checked when you crossed the border to Ohio. You might not be able to use your Pennsylvania license plates in New Jersey. Your sneakers, which were acceptable footwear at home, might keep you out of a New York McDonald's for lunch. When back in the safe territory of your home state, you might retaliate by refusing to give out-of-state visitors directions to the highway, by making them show four photo I.D. cards before cashing their checks in your store, or by laughing at their misspelling of Pittsburgh.

When your stepfamily first begins, the boundaries around each of the minifamilies seem to impose the same kinds of absurd restrictions on members of other minifamilies. These boundaries keep you at a safe emotional distance from the other minifamilies and prevent you from feeling that you are a member of the stepfamily as a whole. These boundaries are enforced by both the children and the adults. Here are some examples:

Your ten-year-old stepson, John, had always been called Jay-Jay by his family. One day you affectionately address him as Jay-Jay and he becomes enraged. *"You* call me John!" he tells you emphatically. You get the message that you are still an outsider.

Your wife is sleeping at 10:30 p.m. after an exhausting day. She is awakened by a phone call from your eight-year-old stepdaughter, who was supposed to be spending the night with a friend but has changed her mind and wants to be picked up. You get out your car keys and are stopped by your drowsy wife, who insists that she needs to fetch her daughter. Your good intentions have bumped into a strong boundary.

Your six-year-old is visiting you for the weekend. He and your husband's children are watching television quietly on Saturday morning, and you think this is a good time to get some work done in the yard. Through the open window, you hear your son asking to change the channel. His stepsister answers, "We don't like that show and it's our house, so we win." Your son, now in tears, has just been reminded that he is on the other side of a firm minifamily boundary.

The Outer Boundary

It is the strength of the boundaries between the minifamilies which reminds you that you are not a member of a big, united family. In contrast, the boundary that separates the stepfamily from the rest of the community is flexible and flimsy. Your house seems to have a revolving door. In come your stepchildren for a weekend visit. Out go your children to see their father. In comes your ex-husband to pick up the hockey equipment your son forgot. Out goes your stepson to be with his friends. In comes your husband's ex-wife, returning your stepson from a movie. Out goes your husband to take his kids somewhere special. You may feel that you can't let your hair down and relax because as you await the arrival of your stepchildren you wonder if their other parent, your partner's ex-spouse, is going to come in with them and start chatting.

Not only do you see people come and go frequently, but you also receive many communications from and about your family. You get phone calls from two former spouses, receive report cards from several schools, are asked to provide rummage sale items and baked goods for more fund-raisers than you can keep track of. In some cases, you are talking to your children's and stepchildren's teachers, guidance counselors, or psychotherapists regularly. One night you find yourself calling your husband's ex-wife's brother to relay a change in plans for a visit to be made by your stepchildren.

The finances of your stepfamily are not as separate as those of a nuclear family either. One couple made a chart of the amount of money he was to pay his ex-wife in child support over the next ten years and the amount of money she would be receiving from her ex-husband. Both divorce agreements were written so that the amounts changed each year. The couple realized that in three years the amount coming in from her former husband would equal the amount going out to his former wife. A friend suggested that they take the check from her ex-husband and just endorse it to his ex-wife. Although the couple laughed at this idea, they realized how wonderful it would feel to be financially separate from both former marriages.

Time

Time can also be used to form and maintain boundaries. The negotiations with your former spouse over child time and nonchild time are now built into the daily life of your stepfamily.

When your ex-husband tells you, in a sacred tone, that this Friday night he wants to have some "alone time" with his son, who will be visiting for the weekend, you feel as though a door has been shut in your face. And it has. Even if the three of you are in the house together, the definition of alone time will serve as an invisible wall between you.

The custody and visiting arrangements set up certain patterns of time membership in your family. One father-stepfather described a typical week in his home:

> Saturday night we are home alone. Sunday night my two kids come back from their mother's, so we are four. Monday, Jean's daughter returns from her father's after school, and we are five until Thursday. Then my kids go back to their mother's, and we are three until Saturday. Each week we build up to a crescendo when we are all here and then calm down again in stages.

The time arrangements of the divorce are then complicated by the needs of the individuals and minifamilies in the stepfamily. You want some time alone with your wife. Your son wants you to spend time helping him with his pitching. Your stepdaughter wants her mom to take time to help her plant a garden. You and your wife want to have more family time when all of you are together. If you're a typical remarried parent, you have no time to yourself. If you take off one weekend a year to play golf, both your children and wife gang up on you. You find yourself jogging at 6 a.m. because it's the only time when no one misses your presence in the house. You wonder how you can all feel like a regular family when your existence is ruled by the clock and the calendar.

VISITING

Visiting children often have the most resistance to accepting the new stepfamily. They feel excluded because so much of stepfamily life goes on without them. When they are there, they often want time to be with their biological parent apart from the other stepfamily members, enforcing a minifamily boundary. We have seen that the visits, and the transitions before and after, are confusing to the members of the visiting minifamily. The visits and transitions also affect the lives of the other stepfamily members.

As a stepparent (with or without children of your own), you may not be able to avoid feeling the tension your wife or husband feels as a visit approaches. The tension arises because he or she fears rejection by the children. You may get caught up in the planning. Where can you take them? What kind of food should you buy? If you also have children, you may try to plan an event for the whole family. By the time the children arrive, neither of you is calm.

During the visit, you are aware that your partner is very involved with his or her children and has less emotional energy for you. You can't tell what he is thinking or feeling. He changes his behavior, talks differently, in some kind of accent he thinks the children understand. Or she watches TV movies she would never sit through if you suggested them. The feeling of being an outsider becomes stronger.

After the visit, you may have no idea how it went. Did you pull it off? A weekend that may have seemed fine to you could have been very upsetting to your spouse: "The children weren't themselves." Or one that seemed disastrous to you could have been fine for her. After the visitors have left, when you expect your partner to reconnect with you, he or she is often recovering physically and emotionally from the strains of the visit.

Everyone involved in the visit can have a different agenda. If we could list the agendas a little more honestly than most family members ordinarily would, they might look like this:

WILL (the dad to be visited): Have a good talk with Jim about grades. Try to listen to Erica. Help Helen see they're not such bad kids.

HELEN (stepmother of visiting children): Keep Will in a good mood. Don't let the kids manipulate us into driving them all over. Spend some time with Katie (her daughter) and with Will. Sign Father's Day cards to the grandfathers.

JIM: Meet friends who will be hanging out at Oak Hill Mall. Sleep late. Keep Dad from giving me one of his lectures.

ERICA: Talk Dad into letting me go on a cross-country bicycle trip this summer. See if he'll pay at least half. Keep Katie out of my room and try to be nicer to Helen, for Dad's sake.

KATIE: Get Erica to fix my hair for me and let me use her nail polish. Go shopping with Mom for summer clothes. Tease Will to get some attention.

It is obvious from looking at this partial list that some of the agenda items fit together nicely (Katie's desire to go shopping matches Helen's desire to spend time with Katie, if money is not a major problem) and others clash directly (Will's plan to talk to Jim about grades and Jim's wish to avoid lectures from his dad).

Some agenda items are likely to have the support of an entire minifamily (Will, Jim, and Erica, based on their history and expectations, are likely to agree about the bicycle trip, for example) and not have the support of another minifamily (Helen thinks Erica should earn some of the money for such an expensive trip and was hoping that Will's kids would come with them to their lakeside cottage; Katie will agree with Helen). Items such as signing the Father's Day cards are likely to be acceptable to the entire minifamily as long as Helen has already picked out the cards and doesn't expect the children to take any initiative in locating addresses or buying stamps. Two of the three minifamilies may oppose the idea of having Helen and Will spend time together; the children would rather have the parents available to them. Even Jim, who wants to get out to see his friends, will want his dad to give him a ride to the mall or be home when he comes in.

You may be thinking that a nuclear family with three children could have just as many diverse agenda items on a typical weekend. You are right. There are, however, some significant differences. Take the issue of Jim's grades, for example. Will feels especially tense about this because his ex-wife has been critical of him for not being more involved with Jim's school. Will feels guilty because he has not attended parent-teacher conferences or even seen a report card in several years. Moreover, he cannot choose the best time to talk about this problem but must force the issue to come up over the weekend. He knows this will lead to conflict, which he would also rather avoid on the one weekend a month he has his children around.

In a nuclear family, Will would have many more opportunities to discuss the grades, would have been involved in the problem sooner, and would be able to balance the difficult confrontation with a supportive connection at another time. In addition, he does not have the same kind of support from Helen on this issue that he would have from Jim's mother. If Helen does enter the conversation, Jim may feel resentful that she is "butting in."

Coping with transportation and transitions is part of stepfamily life too. When you are a divorced visiting parent, arrangements for the children's visits are confined to your ex-spouse and your children. This can be hard enough. When you are remarried, these same plans must be cleared with your new spouse and sometimes with your stepchildren. If your children or your former spouse change the plans at the last minute, *you* are going to receive the anger of your new family members.

If you feel sad after you take your children back at the end of your time with them, when you're a single visiting parent, you can think over the visit, have a good cry in the car, stop at a favorite bar or restaurant on the way home, or space out in front of the TV. When you're remarried, you will probably be accompanied by part of your new family for the return trip or you will be expected at home to join in plans that are already made. Your spouse has been feeling left out and wants a little special time with you before the busy week starts.

You may think things will get easier when your children are finally old enough to transport themselves to your house unescorted. However, adolescents may be less responsible than you would like. One teenager who missed the Friday bus to her father's after school went to a phone booth to tell him she would be late. When the line was busy, she spent her change on a soda. All she had left was her bus ticket. Her father, waiting at the terminal, became worried when she wasn't on the usual bus. Her stepmother and two half-sisters were waiting dinner for her. The visitor, when she finally arrived, could not understand her father's anger and her stepmother's coldness. Weren't they glad to see her?

A final word about visits. What does it mean when the child refuses to come? Parents and stepparents easily form their own conclusions when a child chooses not to visit or avoids visiting by being ill, getting a part-time job, or making other plans. You feel rejected and hurt. Your own child or your stepchild does not want to see you. Consider some other reasons why children, or a particular child, may be avoiding visits:

- They may feel so pressured by the custodial parent, either not to visit or to act as a spy, that they do not feel comfortable in your home.

- The custodial parent may be so depressed that the children are afraid to leave him or her alone.

- The custodial parent may be in a relationship with someone who is abusive, and the children may feel they have to stick around to protect that parent.

- Your children's feelings may have been hurt, unknowingly, by someone in your household.

- They may feel intimidated by you or your spouse or teased by the other children.

- Maybe they think you will not allow their friends to visit.

What can you do when your children do not want to visit?

1. Become a detective to find out the real reason why.

2. Let your children know that you are open to talking about their feelings and that you are willing to consider making changes if there are some problems between you.

3. Be firm and persistent in expressing your desire to see them. You are the adult. If you are spiteful and rejecting to your children because you feel hurt, you are definitely making the situation worse. Your children need to know that you are so strong and love them so much that you will continue to care even when they are acting stubborn and distant.

4. Don't sulk. Spend time with your spouse and stepchildren instead, or do what interests you. Your children do not benefit

from your being in a bad mood during the time they are supposed to visit.

5. When they finally or eventually do come, don't say how disappointed you were by their absence. That is sure to lead to
fewer visits in the future.

6. If you think there is a reason for concern about the child's
well-being in either home, or if you want some professional
help, consult a counselor or psychotherapist. An experienced
third party can sometimes help you communicate and get
your stuck relationship moving again.

CHILDREN'S ADJUSTMENTS

For children, the remarriage is another change. It's not usually a
change they want. They have just recently begun to feel comfortable in the single-parent minifamily. Now you're asking them to get
used to another person living in your house, taking you away from
them and bringing in other children for weekly visits. You've got to
be kidding.

Children can grow immensely from your remarriage. They are
often better cared for, better supervised, freer to act their age, and
happier in stepfamilies. You must not expect them to say so,
though, or to imagine that they will.

Your children have two major motives for resisting your remarriage:

1. They are loyal to the former nuclear family and the two parent-child minifamilies they have. Their loyalty prevents them
from accepting the new stepfamily.

2. They don't like changes that are imposed by you.

Loyalty

Loyalty is usually considered a praiseworthy quality. A loyal em-
ployee is valued. Loyal citizens are honored. Loyal sons and
daughters are cherished. It is only when you are trying to transfer
allegiances from the parent-child minifamily—or the nuclear

family—to the new stepfamily that loyalty gets in the way of acceptance.

Children are very loyal creatures. Their primary loyalties are to each of their parents. They will even act in ways that are opposed to their own growth and development in order to be loyal to other family members. One little boy refused pancakes (his favorite breakfast) made by his stepmother because he felt that eating her pancakes would be disloyal to his mother. Another child went to a movie she had already seen three times because that was the choice of her sister. The film she really wanted to see was being suggested by her stepbrother, and she was not ready to be counted on his side in the family vote. Family therapists have found that behavior such as lying, truancy, and bed-wetting can be the expression of a young child's loyalty.

Parents are also loyal to their children. In Chapter Three it was Ted's loyalty to his children, and to the minifamily they had established together, that led him to hold on so long to his own apartment as the place for entertaining his children.

Just as you have an image of the ideal family, your child or stepchild has a picture of what a family is; this picture rarely contains two mothers or two fathers. When children are not ready to accept the new stepparent or stepfamily, it is often because they consider accepting them a sign of disloyalty to the previous family. The more you can convince your children that your new wife is not trying to replace their mother, or that your new husband is not trying to replace their father, the less the children will feel they are being asked to be disloyal. The more you can respect your children's loyalty to your former spouse, the more they will be able to be loyal to you as well.

WEDDING BELLS

Children of the bride and groom can add a sense of warmth and charm to the wedding. They can be cute or elegant; they can add a touch of spontaneous humor. Children welcoming a new stepparent into their family at the wedding ceremony can bring tears to the assembled guests.

Don't count on it. If your children have agreed to be part of the ceremony, they may back out at the last minute. One twelve-year-old couldn't be in the wedding party because her dress got too wrinkled in the car on the way to the church. If your children don't want to be in the ceremony, don't pressure them, but do try to keep a spot open in case they change their minds.

In the weeks and days before the wedding the children may be sad, tearful, and withdrawn. One boy told his father to get married "in the doghouse." They may arrive the day before the wedding in torn blue jeans and tennis shoes that look more like sandals with not a thought about what they will be wearing for the big event. Or they may pester you for new and expensive clothes from head to foot.

Children at their parents' weddings have been known to eat too much, drink too much, and cry too much. They try to be the center of attention; they talk about the parent who is not present, start arguments with their friends, get cranky, and flirt with relatives of the new stepparent. Young children often have a hard time keeping themselves together on special occasions because they become overexcited and overtired. The parent's wedding may also be a symbol of a change to which they are not looking forward.

Here are some simple suggestions if you are planning a second marriage:

- Do include the children.

- Assign a relative or friend whom the children know to keep an eye on them so you are not torn between being the star of the show and being the baby-sitter. If the children are young, or the party will go on quite late, arrange for them to have a ride home at an appropriate time.

- If the wedding is to be followed by a honeymoon, be sure you say good-bye to the children and reassure them of your plans to return to them.

- If the children have a role in the ceremony, keep it simple, have an adult who is there to guide them, and have a backup plan in case they fall apart.

- Don't count on the other parent to provide the children with appropriate outfits. Buy them clothes, or help them choose from their wardrobes, and set the wedding clothes aside a few weeks in advance.

- Be very clear about what will happen and what you expect from them.

- Don't push the children into the spotlight. A few pictures of them would be a good touch, but remember that this is your day.
- Don't let the children get between you and your new spouse in any way. They may try.

Most children, as morose as they are about the wedding in its planning stages, enjoy a party. When they see your (and their) friends and relatives congratulating you and having a good time, they will most likely join in the fun. If they do not, don't try to cheer them up. They need to work through their own feelings, which are different from yours.

Changes in Daily Life

When Marge and Ned married, his son Jeff was ten and his daughter Belinda was twelve. Marge's son Robbie was fifteen and her daughter Miriam was thirteen. When the four children were together, Belinda went from being the only girl in her family and the oldest child to being one of two girls and the third oldest. Miriam also lost her place as the only girl and the youngest in her mini-family.

Family positions are important to children, and they miss them when things change. They are used to behaving like the big sister or the family baby and being treated accordingly.

Ned's children spent the summers and every other weekend during the school year with Ned. Marge's children spent every other weekend with their father. Ned and Marge arranged to coordinate their schedules so that one weekend all four children would be with them and the next all four children would be out of the house. Plans for those weekends when all the children were there often focused on Jeff and Belinda. When would they be picked up? Would the family do something special together? A den had to be converted to a bedroom for them. One Friday afternoon Miriam, Marge, and Robbie were arranging the house to accommodate the other two children. Miriam became very angry. "These are our only weekends with you, Mom," she said, "but we seem to spend them doing all these special things for Jeff and Belinda. Why don't you ever think about what we want? Why are these always called the weekends that Ned's kids are coming, not the weekends when your kids are staying?"

Competition and jealousy among the stepchildren are almost inevitable. The visiting children are jealous because their stepsiblings get to be with their father more often than they do. The custodial children are jealous of the energy expended to please the visitors. As we have already seen, the children's agendas for their time in the stepfamily may be very different. The children who are biological brothers or sisters may show loyalty to each other by being unfriendly to the steprelations.

As parents, we expect a lot of our children when we ask them to be part of a stepfamily. We ask them to share bedrooms, do chores together, relax together, and share in the celebration of birthdays and holidays. When they cannot meet our demands, we are upset even though the members of the stepfamily are nearly strangers to our children. Our fondness for the offspring of a new spouse is not transferable to our children.

The children's ages make a difference. Young children may be able to accept each other more easily because they are less particular about their friends. Older children and adolescents may think that the stepbrother or stepsister is someone they ordinarily would never like. They may not want their friends to know that this person is now in their family.

When one set of children are much older than the other, the reasons for jealousy are reduced. The little children need a different kind of attention. A four-year-old doesn't mind if you extend the sixteen-year-old's curfew, but a fourteen-year-old does. The sixteen-year-old isn't jealous when you pick up the four-year-old and put him on your lap; the six-year-old is. A big difference in ages, however, means that the family gatherings are stilted. Your sixteen-year-old feels like the baby-sitter when your husband's four-year-old and six-year-old go on the swings in the park. You feel like the baby-sitter when your husband leaves you with his little children so he can shoot baskets with your big one.

Two children in a stepfamily can be the same age but very different in personality or maturity. In one family a six-year-old girl was reading and writing at a fourth-grade level and was accustomed to playing with her older brother and sister. Her stepsister, who was also six, had a speech defect and received remedial help in school.

She had difficulty making friends. The child who was more mature was jealous of the ways in which her stepsister received special attention from the adults, and the one who was less mature felt inadequate when she saw what her stepsister could do.

Benefits

Despite all this shifting and difficulty in finding one's right place in the stepfamily, stepbrothers and stepsisters often do like each other and learn from each other. They can watch as the older or more skillful children handle their parents' moods, their own friendships, and their schoolwork. They can form allegiances against the adults and ask each other for support in getting a special favor or changing a family rule. They learn about places they have never been, hear music they have never heard, and meet people whom they never would have met. They get a view of another family's divorce through the eyes of another child or set of children.

Sometimes the children are very giving to each other and appreciate the extension of the family resources. One twelve-year-old who was eight years older than his half brother (at his dad's) and six years younger than his stepsister (at his mom's) described these relationships:

When I am at Dad's I don't know why Ronnie likes me so much. He always wants to play with me. When I go back to Mom's and Fran visits, I see how much I like her and want to do things with her. I guess that's how Ronnie feels about me.

CHAPTER SIX

Stage Two: Authority

Your stepfamily has reached the *authority stage* when:

- The number of loud arguments in your house increases
- As a stepparent, you are putting your foot down with your stepchildren more often
- As a biological parent, you are not interfering when your spouse disciplines your children
- Your stepchildren, who have been quiet and polite, are beginning to challenge your authority
- You and your spouse are talking about how to handle the children and how to coordinate your actions

The authority stage is the make-it-or-break-it stage for many stepfamilies. Stepfamily couples who seek counseling often do so at the time they are facing issues of power and authority. The authority stage often occurs between one and three years after the remarriage. Forty percent of the marriages that end in divorce do so before the fourth year.[1] Unresolved authority issues have probably contributed to the second divorce. Stepfamilies that survive this stage in their development seem able to remain together.

The question of authority—who's in charge—comes up in every family. In your first marriage, the power struggles were between you and your spouse. When you had children, no one questioned your right to discipline them. You may have disagreed with your partner or your children about establishing the rules, but you knew the adults had the right to enforce them.

In the stepfamily, children growing up in two different minifamilies have never known their stepparents as adult authorities. They do not automatically transfer the respect and obedience they give their parent to a stepparent. Even children as young as four or five can be staunch challengers of the stepparent.

During the acceptance stage of your stepfamily, each minifamily tries to keep its own way of doing things. You do not want to interfere with your wife's way of raising her kids. (In Chapter Four, we advised you not to.) You don't know what your role is in setting limits for the children. You let her deal with them as much as possible. She keeps out of your minifamily too.

If your family were to continue in this manner indefinitely, you would have some serious handicaps. You would be running two parallel families in the same house, but you wouldn't be working together. Your decision making would be chaotic. The children would have different rules and chores. You and your wife would never discuss some of your differences. There would be a very good chance of resentments building up. Your family would not become more unified, and it would not be likely that you could get close to your stepchildren.

Many stepfamilies do get stuck in avoidance of the authority stage. If your stepfamily is stuck, you are likely to run out of patience. When you do, you may either leave the marriage or push your entire stepfamily into the authority stage by demanding change.

The moment of transition came for Ned (of Ned, Jeff, and Belinda and Marge, Robbie, and Miriam) the twenty-fifth time he had to move Robbie's bike from his parking spot on the driveway. Twenty-four times he had left his car, moved the bike, and then parked the car. He had mentioned it very politely to Marge and to Robbie. Robbie had nodded that he heard, and Marge had told Robbie she expected him to remember in the future.

On this particular Friday when the bike was there again, the temperature was 90 degrees. Ned was an hour late because he had been in a colossal traffic jam. He was looking forward to a peaceful weekend with his wife when he remembered, as he turned the corner of their street, that her kids were not going to their father's as usual because Robbie was staying to participate in a big Saturday morning swim meet. He was swallowing his disappointment as he turned into the driveway and saw the bike there again. His first impulse was to smash right into it. Instead, he parked his car on the street and stormed into the house.

"Young man," he shouted at Robbie, "if you don't move that bike in ten seconds, it will be smashed to smithereens."

He threw his car keys at Marge. After all, Robbie was her child. "And you can go move my car into the shade after he does it. I've had it with being nice to your sloppy kid."

As Ned stripped off his sweaty clothes and went into the shower, he had only two regrets: that he had not exploded sooner and that his own children were not there to see him. They always said he was easier on Marge's kids than on them.

Ned's double outburst of anger, at his stepson and at his wife, was very revealing. The authority stage requires a change in both the couple relationship and the relationship between stepparents and the stepchildren. In this case, Robbie was less disturbed by the outburst than Marge. Robbie realized that his stepfather had every right to be annoyed. He moved his bike, apologized sheepishly later that evening, and didn't give it another thought as he prepared himself for the swim meet. If Ned had yelled at him in this way much earlier in the marriage, Robbie might have been resentful. He might have asked, "What gives you the right to yell at me?" or retorted, "You're not my father; you can't tell me what to do." But Ned's record as a stepfather who was kind and helpful had earned Robbie's acceptance. It had earned Ned the right to a good yell now and then.

Marge was more resistant to accepting Ned's right to discipline her son. She said the children had heard more than enough yelling from their own father. Actually, she felt frightened by open expressions of anger. She was nearly in tears as she moved Ned's car, too intimidated not to do what he demanded. She feared that anger could turn into violence. She and Ned sometimes had private arguments, but so far they had been able to resolve their differences fairly civilly. Was this the beginning of the end?

During the authority stage, two very important changes take place in the stepfamily system:

1. The new couple becomes the most powerful minifamily in the stepfamily.

2. Each adult assumes authority over all the children from each marriage.

THE AUTHORITY OF THE COUPLE

When the stepfamily begins, the couple minifamily has less status and seniority than the parent-child minifamilies. Take Ned and Marge's family, for example. Marge had been a single parent for five years before she married Ned. Ned had been a visiting parent for three years. They had known their own children from birth, and the youngest child was ten when they married. Ned and Marge had known each other for only a year and a half before their marriage. Their minifamily was a baby compared to the other minifamilies in the stepfamily. Your short history as a couple means that you are just learning to work together when you begin the joint enterprise of parenting two sets of children.

Many parents protect their children from a new spouse. As happy as you are when your partner helps your child with homework, teaches her how to swim, or offers her a ride to a birthday party, you are not pleased when the stepparent criticizes her table manners, reprimands her for her messy room, or punishes her for misbehavior. Your instinct as a parent is to jump in between your child and your spouse and say, "Don't you speak to my child that way."

Your reaction makes sense. After all, for the last several years you have been the sole adult in charge of your children. Now you have to start behaving like one half of a new team. Your allegiance has to shift to your marriage. You need to consider the opinion of your new spouse and allow him or her to deal with your children directly. You have to restrain yourself from protecting the children unless you feel they are being abused or strongly misunderstood.

The stepparent's authority must be backed up by a strong and united couple. If a parent-child minifamily can overrule the couple, the stepparent is apt to be undermined by the child's appeal to the biological parent for protection from the stepparent. The stepparent will never gain authority.

Marge's parent-child minifamily, in our example, had resisted Ned's authority. Although Robbie and Marge had heard Ned's complaints about the driveway, they had not taken him too seriously. Robbie, suspecting that his mother thought Ned was making a fuss about nothing, had not bothered to change his habits. It could be that he resented leaving the parking space for his mother's new husband and that Marge was unconsciously flattered by her son's desire to stand between his mother and another man.

Ned made two clear demands—that Robbie obey him and that Marge enforce his authority with Robbie. He had to confront his stepson directly because his wife was not checking on Robbie's responsibility for the bike. He knew, however, that without his wife's support, Robbie would probably continue to ignore his requests.

COUPLE VULNERABILITY

Sharing the management of your stepfamily makes your couple relationship more vulnerable. You have to face differences that you may have been avoiding until now. You fear that one disagreement can mean the end of your second marriage. You may be aware of a problem area, but you don't bring it up because you cannot imagine how you and your husband can reach an agreement. You may tell yourself, "As long as I'm not in charge of his children, I'll live with things the way they are. It's better than having an argument."

There is another paradox you may encounter if you take the risk of confronting your partner. Talking about differences and, especially, listening to each other will help you grow closer.

Marge, for example, spent the first year of her marriage to Ned trying gently and subtly to convince Ned to set bedtimes for Jeff and Belinda. He would agree on 9 o'clock for Jeff and 9:30 for Belinda. On the next weekend visit, both children would again be up past 10 o'clock watching television or playing cards in the den. If Marge asked Ned why they were still up, he would say he had given them special permission or was going to tell them in a minute or he had forgotten the time.

Finally, after Marge had survived Ned's throwing the car keys, she got up the courage to confront him. "You say your kids have bedtimes when they're here, but I've never seen you remind them to go to bed, and they are always up later than their bedtimes. What's going on?"

Ned, feeling powerful after his incident with Robbie, told Marge his true opinion about bedtimes for the first time: "I don't believe in bedtimes. When they're tired, they go to bed. I don't see my kids that much. I want them to have a good time. I don't want to be a jailer when they're here; I want to be their father."

"Then why did you say you'd set bedtimes?"

"I guess I didn't want to let you down. It seemed so important to you."

Marge felt that Ned had deceived her by agreeing to something on which he was not intending to follow through. Ned thought he was being a good husband by trying to please her. It took a long time for each to see the other's point of view. When they did, Marge could appreciate Ned's genuine desire to honor her wishes even though they were not his, and Ned could see how saying one thing and doing another did not please his wife. They were then able to talk more openly about bedtimes and to agree on some rules for the children's visits. They planned a family meeting with all the children to explain the rules and agreed that either Ned or Marge could remind the children when necessary.

In this discussion Ned and Marge began to work as a parental team. Although they had to have many such talks over the next few months to clarify their points of view, they felt better about themselves as a couple because they were talking honestly. They found the courage to disagree with each other and discovered that the sky didn't fall when they did.

It is not easy to work out differences about child rearing with your new spouse. Your children are a topic as close to your heart as you can get. You have been doing your best to take care of them under trying circumstances, and you don't want criticism from anyone—not even your husband or wife. How can you reveal your doubts and inadequacies? What if you have already made too many mistakes? Can you really trust your partner when he says he cares about your children? Can you trust yourself when you say you care for his?

Here are some guidelines for working on these issues:

- You and your partner need lots of time to become a parenting team. It may be harder in your second marriage because you have already formed habits and opinions. Don't expect to resolve your differences easily or quickly. The first step is learning what the differences are. It is easier to acknowledge that you disagree than to give lip service to something you really can't support.

- Learn to listen to your partner carefully. Instead of preparing an answer in your mind while she is talking, think about what she is saying. Ask her why she feels that way, how her way worked for her in her first marriage or as a single parent. Sometimes, reviewing her own thinking with a good listener will help her recognize something that is not working.

- Perhaps you think your wife is being too strict about the children's chores. In your discussion she concludes, "Maybe I just expect too much of them. They're only kids." You have made your point without opposing her. Now you can help her loosen up. If she does come up with the very criticism that has been in your mind, don't say, "I told you so. That's just what I've been trying to say for the last month." If you do, she's apt to take it back. Just give her support for being honest with you.

- If you are being criticized by your partner, try to listen to the criticism before you defend yourself. Consider the minute possibility that there is a grain of truth in what the other person is saying. Ask him for evidence that you are too strict and that the children are afraid when you yell at them. How does he know that other children their age don't have so many chores? If you think he has a point and you can't admit that you have been wrong, you don't have to say anything right away. Tell him you have to think it over. Say he might be right. Ask him, "What would you do instead?"

- If you are a stepparent who is not also a parent, you still have the right to express your feelings about the children's behavior, your criticism of your spouse, and your expectations for change. Trust your gut feelings about the children and the family. Listen to what your partner has learned from his experiences with the children, but don't let yourself be pushed into giving up your ideas. You may have a lot to offer.

- Don't have a discussion about your differences if you're extremely tired or grumpy or angry about something else. You will never resolve anything. It's fair to say you'll talk about something later as long as you are willing to find another time.

- Remember that you don't have to agree on everything. Most other couples live with their differences, and so can you. A disagreement does not mean another divorce.

- Don't be surprised if one of you becomes angry. If there were no problem, you wouldn't be talking. Attempting to share the care of your children with another adult is risky. Your ability to trust is on the line. Your deepest feelings are aroused because you love your children and your partner.

- Exposing your pain, hurt, doubts, fears, and worries can be great. Forget all your training in "being a man," "keeping a stiff upper lip," and "smiling no matter what." This is the person with whom you have chosen to share yourself. That means saying how much it hurts to drive your son back to his father's after a visit. It means crying. It means saying how much pain you feel when your son ignores your wife or her daughter ignores you.

- If your partner is sharing some of these deep feelings, you may feel embarrassed and not know how to respond. Just say, "I didn't know you felt that way," or "I can see how you'd feel like that," or "That must really be hard for you." Recognizing her feelings helps you grow closer. Being recognized helps you feel trust. You don't have to have the same feelings as she does.

- Feelings do not follow the rules of logic. You can never convince someone that his feelings are wrong. You may think it strange that he reacts the way he does. You can try to change what he does about those feelings.

- Don't pressure yourselves to come up with a solution. The first step is to define the problem and share the feelings you have about it. Sometimes you need a few days to recover from exposing your feelings to your partner before you can talk about nuts and bolts. Sometimes just talking about the problem brings you a sense of relief.

LEADERSHIP

As the couple's power as a minifamily increases, they take on the leadership of the stepfamily. Your interests and beliefs determine the stepfamily's lifestyle. You can take all the children to church, become active in community affairs, or plan a vacation in the wilderness. You can limit the amount of time the television set is on, insist that the children do more chores, or sign them up for swimming classes at the Y.

Now you have someone to help you devise strategies to use with your children. Let's suppose that you and your husband have decided that a move to a more rural area would be good for all of you. Your husband, who works in a large industrial park outside the city, could reverse-commute from the country and miss most of the traffic. You work at home and are longing for peace and quiet during the day. In nice weather you could work outside. The children could have more freedom in the country. You wouldn't worry about the busy streets. They could finally get the dog they've been wanting.

Despite these advantages to them, you know that both your children and your husband's will be upset by the move. Your children will have to go to new schools and make new friends. Your stepchildren will have to travel farther to come for their visits. You are asking them to make another major change in their lives.

If you were still a single parent, you might not have the energy to make this move, and you certainly would not have the stamina to convince your children that the move could benefit them. As a couple, you can give each other support. When one of you is tempted to give up the whole project, the other becomes optimistic. You are sure you'll never find the right house, and your husband takes over calling real estate agents. His children are driving him crazy, and you sit down and talk with them one more time.

The move has meaning in your marriage also. You are demonstrating that your marriage is working because you do have the power and the energy to choose the way you want to live. Your children can learn a lot from your example.

Making your couple the most powerful minifamily in your stepfamily is a process. It doesn't happen in one afternoon or one week. It starts with the plans for your wedding and continues for years. Don't be discouraged if it seems to be taking a long time. You are asking each other to change some of your behavior and some of your gut reactions to the children. You are asking the children to give up some of the power they have had in their minifamilies. Change in families often comes in spurts, when you least expect it. A large gain one week may be offset by backsliding the next. This kind of up-and-down progress is predictable.

STEPPARENT AUTHORITY

As a stepparent, you enter the stepfamily with very little authority over the children who are not yours. Initially you may hold back from disciplining them. Eventually you have to move into the role of parental authority. You will know this when your temper boils over, as Ned's did, when your spouse asks you for more help, or when you find you are taking more responsibility with the children. The more you and your partner work together, the easier it will be. However, even with support and coaching from your spouse, there are times when you have to face the children alone.

If you have never had children of your own or worked with children, you may feel you are not qualified to be a stepparent. You don't have any experience or self-confidence. You may be reassured to learn that parents often find it hard to discipline their own children and, despite their years of experience, find it harder yet to deal with stepchildren.

The biological parent's authority is based on the mutual love between parent and child. Yelling at your own child does not decrease the love that you feel. You know that you are setting limits for the child's own good. It is much harder to say no to your stepchild. When you aren't sure of your love for the child (as many stepparents are not), you wonder where the line is between being a stepparent and being a tyrant. Will the friendship you have with the child survive a confrontation?

You may dislike criticizing your stepchild so much that you wish he would never do anything wrong. You have been reminding your own children to pick up their dirty clothes and straighten their rooms for ten years; it's second nature. Reminding your stepson makes you feel uncomfortable. What tone of voice should you use? Should you nag or say please? What does his father expect from him? Your lack of confidence makes you even more annoyed when your stepson does leave his room a mess. It would certainly be much easier for you if he were perfect.

As a parent, you know your children like the back of your hand. Geraldine is whining because she's forgotten to eat her lunch. Instead of sending her to her room to cool off, you sit her down with a peanut butter sandwich and a glass of milk. In ten minutes she'll be herself again. Stepchildren are more mysterious. Does whining mean that they're tired or that they're being obnoxious? When you remind them to make their beds and they forget, are they picking a fight or are they scatterbrained in the morning? You can't expect to get answers to your questions about your stepchildren until you start dealing with them directly.

Becoming an authority with your stepchildren means being able to:

- Remind them of their chores and responsibilities
- Make them stop misbehaving
- Answer yes or no when they want permission for something
- Give them advice

Stages of Authority

The move into a position of stepparent authority usually takes place in steps, as shown in the list below. We will look at each step in detail.

Stages of Stepparent Authority

Step One: Being an adviser to the children's parent and not taking a direct role in disciplining them

Step Two: Protecting your rights as a person in the household who needs privacy and consideration

Step Three: Enforcing the rules and standards that your spouse already has established for the children

Step Four: Joining with your spouse to set new guidelines for the children and participating in family discussions about rules and expectations

Step Five: Making spontaneous decisions about the children and being able to enforce new rules and standards

STEP ONE:
BEING AN ADVISER TO THE CHILDREN'S PARENT
AND NOT TAKING A DIRECT ROLE
IN DISCIPLINING THEM

This step is described in Chapter Four. Your role as a New Person in your partner's life or a brand-new stepparent is to accept your stepchildren and let them accept you before you make strong moves. If you are frequently in a position of responsibility for a stepchild during his or her parent's absence, however, you must quickly advance to the next stages.

STEP TWO:
PROTECTING YOUR RIGHTS AS A PERSON
IN THE HOUSEHOLD WHO NEEDS
PRIVACY AND CONSIDERATION

You are always entitled to ask your stepchildren to respect you as a person. You may not like to have them borrow your tape recorder or use your perfume without asking. Letting children know your personal limits is different from telling them how the household will be run.

You may actually find yourself wondering if it is all right to ask your stepson to turn down his stereo because you are going to sleep. Yes, it is, even if he doesn't like it. You will get less flak from him if you don't go on to tell him you dislike the kind of music he plays or how much better he would do his homework without any music at all. You can make it clear that the request is for your benefit, not his.

If you do not let the children know when they have infringed upon your rights or privacy, you are likely to build up an enormous amount of resentment toward them. You may think the children know their stereo is too loud. That is not true. The children do not know your feelings unless you tell them. You cannot assume that other people know your likes or dislikes if you haven't told them directly. You cannot assume that they know, or have been taught, about what you consider the most rudimentary manners. You cannot assume that they'll keep the stereo low tonight just because last night you asked them to turn it down.

Children in each minifamily have been brought up differently. The fact that your children have been taught your standards of behavior does not mean that your stepchildren of the same ages will know or follow the same rules. Your son knows how to take a clear phone message and be courteous to the person on the other end of the line because you have taught him to do it. Your stepdaughter, who is a year older, may not realize that phone messages need to be written down so that other people can read them.

STEP THREE:
ENFORCING THE RULES AND STANDARDS
THAT YOUR SPOUSE ALREADY HAS ESTABLISHED
FOR THE CHILDREN

When you enforce the same rules as the parent, the children (or their parent) cannot object to the specific requests you are making. If you ask your stepdaughter to do her homework before she watches television and she says her father lets her watch TV while she does her homework, you are caught in a power struggle. If you don't know her father's rule, you cannot tell whether she is telling the truth or whether she is just resisting your authority. However, if you remind her to make her bed in the morning and you know she does this every day, she has no grounds for an argument and is more likely to obey.

Don't underestimate the importance of receiving your partner's backup when you are learning to take command of your stepchildren. Having confidence that you are part of a team helps.

Behaving like an authority does not come naturally to everyone. Finding the right tone of voice may take practice. You have to avoid opening a debate about the usefulness of making beds. You need to be firm and definitive. However, you are not a drill sergeant. No one likes to be ordered around.

A classic negative response from your stepchild is, "You're not my father. I don't have to listen to you." Don't let this throw you. It is true that you are not her father. The lack of a genetic link, however, does not excuse her from listening to you. Here are some answers to have ready:

"I'm not your father, but I'm the grown-up in charge now, and I'm reminding you of the rules."

"You do have to listen to me because I'm the man of the house."

If you are very courageous, "I'm your stepfather, and I expect you to listen to me."

If the you're-not-my-parent routine doesn't throw you off balance, it will soon be dropped.

Hints for Discipline: Here are some additional suggestions for handling discipline with children (yours and his or hers):

- Never make a threat you are not willing to carry out. The child may just call your bluff. If you back down, your credibility is lost. If you carry it out, you may all be sorry.

- Don't call children names. If you label your child or stepchild as lazy, he or she has no reason to be quick the next time. You are disapproving of the child's behavior, not the child. One falsehood does not make a child a liar unless you constantly tell her that she is one. Always assume that children can do better.

- Acknowledge your mistakes. You may have misunderstood some information about when your stepdaughter was due home. You may realize you are in a bad mood. You can say, "I am sorry that I yelled so loud but I still want you to put your clothes away."

- Give the child a few seconds or minutes to do what you have asked. We often expect children to obey us immediately. If you can wait a minute to see whether the child is about to do it, you may not have to repeat yourself. You can also ask the child to acknowledge what you have said. When you call someone to set the table and you hear, "Just a minute. I'm putting away my books," you know you have been heard. When the response is silence, you feel ignored.

- Never use more force than you need for the task at hand. You can save the heavy artillery for the big battles. If you start off with a simple request in a quiet voice and you are not taken seriously, you can increase the volume. If you are obeyed, you can feel good that you have asserted your authority so calmly.

- Don't be distracted by a change of subject when there is a task to be done or a misdeed to be discussed. Don't even fall for some juicy gossip about your partner's ex-spouse that you would love to hear.

- Set an example for children by being polite and respectful of them. They like thanks and praise when they have been trying hard. If you don't want to be interrupted by them, don't interrupt them. In the long run, children learn much, much more from *what we do* than from *what we say*.

- Use the backup of the biological parent carefully. If your authority depends on saying, "I'm going to tell your mother how naughty you've been," you are admitting you don't have power in your own right.

- Control your anger. Do not use physical force with your stepchildren. If punishments are necessary, you and your spouse should agree, in advance, on what they will be.

- One way to keep in control when a child is testing the limits is to appear to lose your temper before you actually do. You can stamp your foot and say, "Now I am really mad!" with great vehemence *before* you get that awful feeling inside of you. This will also help keep your blood pressure down.

- Humor is acceptable, even in serious moments, and can sometimes break the tension between you. One stepmother of a young child, when she got angry would say, "I'm so angry, I'm going to turn you into a pretzel." The child would look shocked, think about the threat, and then laugh. The laughter would shake him out of his stubbornness.

- Don't push the child into a corner. Sometimes giving the child a choice such as, "Do you want to get into your pajamas now or in five minutes?" helps him feel he has some control over the process of getting ready for bed.

- Young children still respond to what used to be called reverse psychology ("You better not eat those peas") and challenges ("I bet you can't put on your own shoes and socks"). Don't try these tactics with anyone over the age of six.

- Talk to other parents and stepparents of children the same age. You may learn that behavior you considered a personal affront is typical for the child's age and is just as annoying to biological parents as it is to you.

Children's Differences: If you are familiar with children because you are an uncle, a teacher, or a camp counselor, you may be surprised that your stepchild does not warm up to you or obey you as children have in your past experience. Suppose you wanted to do some problem solving about this. You list all the possible reasons why your six-year-old stepson, Jason, does not seem to like you or listen to you as much as the other six-year-olds you have known.

1. I have lost my touch.
2. He hates me.
3. His father is poisoning him against me.
4. He is not as mature as other six-year-olds.
5. He is depressed.
6. He is working through the divorce.
7. He hopes his parents will remarry each other.
8. He thinks liking me and obeying me will make him disloyal to his dad.

As you look over this list, you realize that there may be more than one reason for his behavior. Your next step is to pick out the most likely reasons and look at them closely.

I have lost my touch (number 1) would be your conclusion only if all the other reasons were invalid. You set that one aside for now. *He hates me* (number 2) has to be set aside for lack of evidence. Even if he says he hates you, he could mean many different things by this statement. *His father is poisoning him* (number 3) is the coward's way out: It is tempting to put the blame on someone you barely know. Even if it is so, there are still ways you can alter your stepson's behavior. Put this one aside also.

He is immature, he's depressed, he is working through the divorce (numbers 4, 5, and 6) go together. A divorce experience can interfere with a child's development. Most children catch up to their agemates, but maybe Jason has not yet done so. You start to think of him as a child who, at least temporarily, has special needs. Maybe you have to change your approach to him. Slow down. Be calmer. Watch him for clues.

He wishes his parents would remarry (number 7) and *he fears being disloyal to his father* (number 8) are possible outgrowths of *working through the divorce* (number 6). Most children wish their parents would remarry and most try to be loyal to the absent parent. There's not much you can do about the wish that his parents will remarry. Most children outgrow this desire when they see that it is not about to happen. His mother can help by telling him that she is happy with you. If he asks her questions about remarrying his dad, she can explain the realities of the divorce. You can let him know, by listening when he talks about his dad and by not arguing with his outrageous claims about his father, that you are not asking him to be disloyal. You can even ask him how he knows when his father expects him to listen.

You now have some ideas about what may be causing the problem and some ideas about what to do differently. Your strategy could be to:

1. Watch Jason more closely for signs of wanting or not wanting attention. Avoid strong moves toward him if he is pulling away.

2. Talk to him slowly and explain what you are asking him to do as though he were a little younger. Give him lots of time and encouragement before you blow up, but be firm with him.

3. Talk with his mom and his teachers about how typical his behavior is for a child his age. Ask if they think he's depressed. Find out whether he's coming out of the divorce experience. Ask how they can help.

4. Let Jason know you respect his relationship with his dad.

We began this exercise assuming you felt snubbed by Jason and powerless to control his behavior. You now have a greater understanding of what life might be like for Jason right now, a plan of action that gives you a greater sense of competence, and ideas to share with other people who care about your stepson. By putting aside your sense of rejection and inadequacy (remember numbers 1 and 2) and looking at Jason as an individual, not just another six-year-old, you may be able to take some initiative toward helping Jason listen to you, toward helping him grow up.

If you suspect that your stepchildren are extreme in their behaviors, follow up your hunches and ask your spouse, "Do the kids get out of control more now than they did before the divorce or the remarriage? Did they always cry and snap at each other so much?" Read books about child development; they describe typical behaviors for children of different ages. You can compare your stepchildren's behavior to these norms. You can also talk to other parents.

One stepmother spent several years trying to entertain her adolescent stepchildren after school every day. It was only much later, when they had gone off to live on their own, and her own younger children were teens, that she realized most adolescents do not come straight home from school every day of the week to be with their parents or stepparents. If she had understood adolescence better, she might have been able to help her stepchildren become more involved with their friends, sports, or other activities, and she would have felt less burdened by them.

STEP FOUR:
JOINING WITH YOUR SPOUSE
TO SET NEW GUIDELINES FOR THE CHILDREN
AND PARTICIPATING IN FAMILY MEETINGS
ABOUT RULES AND EXPECTATIONS

As you assert yourself more with your stepchildren and find yourself respected by them, you become ready to take on responsibility for setting rules, not just carrying them out. You don't want to put your foot down for something he or she believes in and you don't. At this stage your direct participation with the children can lead to useful discussions with their parent. You may be able to share information about the children which their parent has not seen or acknowledged.

Your day-to-day experience gives you more information and confidence than you had before. You may think that setting the table is something the younger child could take over. Why can't the ten-year-old help with cleanup? Maybe your stepdaughter has been fresh lately and you want some ideas about how to cope with her. Your husband is bothered by this behavior also. If you agree on the same tactics, you'll have the situation under control more quickly and easily than if each of you deals with her alone.

Your new authority could also lead to more conflicts with your spouse. You are proud that you got the birthday party off to a great start when your husband was late coming back with the pizza, but he feels like a fifth wheel in his own family. Parents who have asked their new partners for help with the kids may be surprised at the resistance they feel when that help is offered and accepted by the children.

Sometimes a parent feels upstaged or demoted when children start listening to another adult. He may think you are too strict or too easy, making too many exceptions to the rules or enforcing them too rigidly. She can object to your tone of voice, your timing, or your ideas for changing things. This is a good time for the two of you to talk, to agree on standards once more, and to reaffirm your cooperation. If you follow the suggestions for discussion as described above, you may come to some new understandings.

Different Standards: If you and your spouse are both parents, you may each have different standards for your own children and for your stepchildren. Parents are often used to putting up with the bad habits they have let their own kids develop but very irritated by the habits of the stepchildren. It makes sense that you have been strictest with your own children about the things that matter most to you. We saw that Marge was not upset when her son left his things around, but Ned was. Ned wasn't bothered when his children stayed up past their bedtimes, but Marge was.

It will take a lot of work to establish nearly the same standards and rules for both sets of children. Whether you feel intimidated when it is time to reprimand your stepchildren or find it easier to yell at them than at your own, you are probably aware that there are differences. You may never eliminate them all.

Some differences in your expectations are based on the differing needs or experiences of the children. You can expect more from your teenager who has always helped you in the kitchen than from your husband's son who has been at boarding school for years. On the other hand, your stepson has better manners than your children.

Ned and Marge seemed to find these differences exaggerated at the times when his children arrived for their visits. Jeff and Belinda would put their things in the den and stay there until they were called for dinner. Marge thought they were very rude not to be friendlier and help set the table. Ned knew they would open up in a few hours and wanted to let them get settled in their own way. Marge's children often criticized their mother for not making their stepsiblings do as much as they did around the house.

Joe, another remarried father, noticed that his new wife was very strict with her children at the dinner table. She expected them to eat neatly, be polite, and behave themselves very properly with adult guests. He was able to relax and enjoy his meals with them. When his own children arrived for their summer visit, however, he became keenly aware that they did not meet his wife's standards. He didn't mind their sloppy table manners and informality. He found himself making excuses for them and trying to soften his wife's criticisms.

You may feel that you have to start over again with your stepchildren to teach them the habits and manners that you have been working on with your kids for many years. Knowing how to clear the table and put away the leftover food is a learned skill, not a behavior that appears at age ten. It requires patience from all of you to apply the same standards for all the children.

Family Meetings: Some stepfamilies have meetings at which they talk about rules, plans, and gripes they have with each other. As the children grow older, it is often helpful to let them become part of the decision-making process. They are more likely to do the chores they have chosen or follow the rules they have agreed are fair than the ones decreed by you. As a stepparent, you are an important participant in these meetings.

A basic rule for family meetings is that some decisions are reserved for the adults. Children can request later bedtimes but cannot vote to stay up until midnight each night. You and your spouse have the final authority. That is your job. You must also set limits on safety issues, such as using the stove when you are not home, crossing busy streets, and walking home alone after dark.

The meetings have three functions. The first one is for everyone to have a chance to express an opinion. Every wish does not become reality, however. The second function is to make decisions in which the children can have equal input. Which of two movies will we go to next week? Is it all right for two of the children to switch beds? The third purpose is for the adults to remind the children what they expect.

If you decide to try such meetings in your home, don't expect them to be popular events. It takes time to feel comfortable telling other people what you want or what bugs you. At first the children may be silent or silly or interrupt each other. However, just having a good meeting can teach all of you a lot about getting along. Once the children know you will really listen to them at meetings, they may begin to use them to talk about what is on their minds.

Both you and your spouse should be leaders at family meetings. One of you is not the chairperson and the other merely the recording secretary. The children need to hear from both of you. You also need to recognize, in front of them, that there are some decisions you will not make until you two, as the executive team of the family, have had a chance for a private conference. The meetings then become another way of enforcing the new hierarchy in your stepfamily.

STEP FIVE:
MAKING SPONTANEOUS DECISIONS ABOUT THE CHILDREN
AND BEING ABLE TO ENFORCE
NEW RULES AND STANDARDS

You are now on your way out of the authority stage. You have passed the tests of enforcement and participation. The children listen to you and respect you. They may sometimes push you more than their parent, or insist on the parent's corroborating that what you say goes, but for the most part you feel confident in laying down the law, and they usually obey you when you do.

When you can respond immediately to a child's phone call asking permission to stay at a friend's for dinner, or to a child who comes home with a note from the teacher saying he has misbehaved, your relationship with the child is more authentic. You and your stepchild have a direct communication line. You also have a greater sense of your own power and authority. By now, you have developed some sensitivity to your stepchildren and your affection for them tempers your decisions. Your spouse trusts you to do what you think is best because you care about what is best for the children.

ADOLESCENT STEPCHILDREN

Adolescence is a time of questioning authority in all families. If you have the good fortune to become the stepparent of a teenager, you may be in for a double dose of resistance. Your stepteen resists you as both a stepparent and an adult. In one study of stepfamilies, stepmothers of teenagers reported more difficulties with their new role than stepparents of younger children.[2]

Teenagers may hassle over the rules as a way of getting to know you. Children's limit testing is a way of trying to grow up, not just a sign of disrespect. They are looking for people to knock up against, and you are a likely candidate. In fact, you may be a safer person to confront than either of their biological parents. They can hate you and still protect their parents from their anger.

Adolescents are often secretly relieved when you put your foot down, regardless of how much they protest. When Ned's stepdaughter, Miriam, tried for half an hour to convince him that she was old enough to hitchhike twenty miles to the beach with her best friend, he resisted tears, shouts, and the threat of two weeks of silent treatment. Ned was able to stick to his guns by imagining Marge (who was away visiting her mother for the day) beating him up if he gave in. Finally, Miriam went sulking to her room. Ten minutes later she was cheerfully taking off on her bike to meet her friend at the town pool. She even blew Ned a good-bye kiss.

Knowing that Ned would say no gave her the safety to act like a big shot and blame her stepfather for not letting her be adventurous. She never had to admit her own fears. Needless to say, Miriam never thanked Ned for keeping her out of danger. Luckily, Marge let Ned know how much she appreciated his excellent parenting.

Adolescents are working hard to increase the emotional distance between themselves and their parents. Resisting authority is one way of becoming more separate. You can help your teenagers by being firm on issues that involve their health and safety and becoming more flexible in areas where you feel they are ready to make their own decisions. Gradually increasing their independence helps them learn to take care of themselves. They know they still have you to fall back on if they mess up.

When seventeen-year-old Perry wanted to quit school two weeks before graduation, his father decided he had to put his foot down. He was surprised that he was supported not only by Perry's stepmother but also by his teenage stepson. His stepson wanted to see Perry protected from the consequences of not having a high school diploma. He also wanted to see if his stepfather would be strong enough to protect him if he got himself into a similar situation.

ANGER

Anger and conflict are tough experiences for most of us. We associate anger with rejection, hurt, and loss. We think of love and anger as opposites. We dread conflict because it can lead to anger.

Stop and think for a minute. Have you ever had a good fight with a friend, heard each other out, made up, and felt better about each other than ever before? Has your respect for a friend or colleague increased when you watched her stick up for herself? Have you and your spouse ever had a good fight followed by passionate lovemaking? If you can answer yes to one of these questions or can think of an experience where anger has resulted in bringing people together, you already know that love and anger can go together.

Anger is frightening because it is a powerful emotion. It can lead to violent feelings and violent actions. But anger that is recognized and controlled is also a sign of personal power and an expression of the depth of our caring. We become most angry at the people we love. If you try to keep anger out of your family life, you are limiting your family's behavior and honesty. If members of your family cannot keep their anger under control and swing at each other, they need help dealing with their violence.

When your stepfamily is working its way through the authority stage, angry feelings are likely to be a common occurrence. Authority issues involve the distribution of power in your family, and anger is an emotion that is aroused when we want to be powerful. Your family will be stronger at this time and in the future if you can:

- Tell each other when you are angry. (You all know it already.)

- Listen to people who are angry at you before you defend yourself or feel guilty. They have a right to their anger even if you did not mean to hurt them.

- Recognize the children's anger. Rather than having temper tantrums, they can learn to share their feelings in ways that you will tolerate. However, don't let their anger become a valid reason for avoiding responsibilities, staying up late, or hitting each other.

- Remember that love and anger can go together. Tell the children you love them even when you are mad at them.

- Learn to understand your own anger. The "Taking a Look at Yourself" exercise in Chapter Five may be helpful for doing this.

- Do not let anger between two people escalate. You don't have to keep fighting. You can end an argument without giving in by saying you don't want to fight any more. Then you will have to resolve your differences in another way at another time.

CHAPTER SEVEN

Stage Three: Affection and Unification

Congratulations are in order for all stepfamilies that have survived the acceptance and authority stages. If you have celebrated your fourth anniversary, you have lasted longer than four-tenths of the couples in second marriages. Although you have come a long way, your stepfamily may still be confusing for these reasons:

- Your stepfamily will never be exactly the same as a nuclear family.
- You and your spouse will always have special feelings for your biological children, as they will for their biological parents.
- From time to time, problems will arise that date back to the previous nuclear family, the divorce, or the remarriage.
- Friends, neighbors, relatives, schools, doctors, and social service organizations may understand less than you do about the special qualities of stepfamilies.

But as you enter the *affection stage* and your family is becoming more unified, you will also find that:

- Members of your family feel more relaxed together.
- The adults are in charge of the family. You operate more like a nuclear family than you have in the past.
- You feel like a family. The members of your family do care about each other.
- Most of the problems and dilemmas you have to face are not a result of being a stepfamily, though being a stepfamily may make solving them harder.
- Your stepfamily is now the background for other events in your life. All your energy is not absorbed in keeping the family together.
- You can feel a sense of pride in the family you have and are creating.

These changes are a result of the passing of time and the creative efforts of you and your family members. You may say you have come this far as the result of luck, the skills of the best family therapist you could hire, or divine intervention (your second marriage was made in heaven, your first was not). But living in a family is not something that just happens to us; it is an active part of our lives, requiring thousands of decisions and lots of energy, caring, and giving. You and your spouse deserve credit for your stepfamily's survival.

CHANGING BOUNDARIES

A major change takes place in the boundaries of your stepfamily during the acceptance and authority stages. The minifamily boundaries become weaker, and the stepfamily develops a new boundary and a new identity. A genuine merger is taking place.

The evidence for this change may sneak up on you. One day you see your two children playing together in their bedroom and your husband's son and daughter in the family room. You wonder what's going on. Usually the two older boys are together and the younger boy and girl. You ask your husband if he thinks there's a problem. Then you both start laughing. A year ago you were concerned because your children and his children were barely on speaking terms. Now you have them grouped into the big kids and the little kids, not mine and yours.

The boundary that separates your couple minifamily from the children becomes stronger. You and your husband rarely need to remind the children not to interrupt when you are having a private talk. They don't protest any more when the two of you go out by yourselves. When you and your husband have plans for the family, his children can't get him to change his mind the way they used to. You are more generous with your stepchildren and more willing to make changes to accommodate their arrangements because that other minifamily is no longer a constant threat to your marriage. And you are less willing to give in to your parent-child minifamily when it interferes with your marriage. The warmth and care your children get in the stepfamily makes up for the closeness you once shared as a minifamily.

Alliances no longer exist primarily between members of the same minifamily. Nearly any combination of family members will get together for a specific purpose. Remember the little girl who chose the movie her sister wanted, even though she had already seen it, because she was being loyal to her minifamily? At this stage in the family development she would probably canvass all family members until she found someone who wanted to go to the same film she did; she would then try to convince the rest of the family to go see it. Her minifamily loyalty would be less important.

These alliances are not permanent. You may join with your stepsons to plan a family fishing trip you know your wife and your daughter are not very enthusiastic about. When the boys want you to take their side in a dispute with their mother about taking a bath, however, you support their mother.

One stepmother noticed how the children's connection with her changed as the stepfamily became more unified:

> Every Saturday morning I went to yard sales to look for things for the basement we were fixing up as a playroom. I would tell the four kids where I was going and ask if anyone wanted to come. For the whole summer and early fall, I could predict who would come—one or both of mine. Then they all came a few times to look for things they could use for Halloween costumes. That was actually my husband's idea—to get them involved in a project together. I was really shocked in the spring when I started going

again and my husband's daughters wanted to come with me and mine couldn't care less. I had arrived. Now I don't go to yard sales as often and it's completely unpredictable who might come with me. Anyone who's up early enough and wants to poke around or have me take them out for a doughnut afterward, I guess.

When the minifamily boundaries are weaker, the children are not crestfallen if their stepmother, not their father, is going to pick them up after gymnastics. They choose to sit next to a stepparent or stepsibling in a restaurant. They introduce each other as brothers and sisters to their friends, call you and your partner "parents," and give all of you birthday presents. One eight-year-old described the change in her feelings about being home with her stepfather and stepbrother.

I didn't like it if Mom left me with Ted [stepfather] and Ricky [stepbrother]. I felt as if Ted was a baby-sitter and he liked Ricky more than me. I wanted to know when Mommy was coming home. Now I still miss Mommy when she's not here, but it's okay to be with Ted and Ricky. They miss Mommy too.

Several years after Marge's son Robbie left his bike in the driveway, he was called into the principal's office to be told that he had received a scholarship to a top college. The principal suggested he phone his folks and tell them the good news. He proceeded to take a slip of paper from his wallet and call four parents, each at his or her workplace. "They're all my folks now," he explained to the secretary as he dialed the last number.

Stepfamily Boundary

While the minifamily boundaries are changing and the parent-child minifamilies are losing their strength, the stepfamily as a whole becomes more coherent and a new and firmer boundary forms around it.

Traditions help to create the new boundary and new identity. If you go away every year for Memorial Day weekend, even children who do not live with you may routinely arrange their time to come that weekend. You celebrate birthdays and holidays together as a family, even if the celebrations are not always on the exact date. You have a favorite pizza shop, a funny nickname for the mailman, a telephone that works only if you hold the wire in place. You all become attached to the little quirks of your family because they define you as unique and special.

Stepfamily History

Your history together is made up of the shared experiences that give you an important connection. When you got a dog, you all had a contest to pick the best name. Now the dog is loved by the members of every minifamily. Your stepson may have been mortified when he threw up in McDonald's on your vacation last year, but now it is a story all the children love to tell and hear. It is part of your history as a stepfamily. Everyone was there when it happened.

Even family disagreements or problems can be looked back upon with a sense of humor and nostalgia:

"Remember that time we threw the spaghetti on the floor and you made us go to bed at 6 o'clock? We used to think you were a mean stepmother."

"Remember how we argued about which Christmas ornaments to use, ours from our old house or yours from your old house, and we ended up going out and getting brand-new ones. Now we seem to find enough places for all of them. How come?"

"Did you really believe I poisoned your coffee when you and Mom just got married? I used to pretend to all the time. I was pretty silly when I was little, wasn't I?"

"Do you know I used to wish I could have a nickel for every time I reminded you kids to say please and thank you. I thought I'd be the richest lady in the country because you never remembered."

"Remember how I cried the day before you and my dad got married? I thought if I cried all night you would call off the wedding and my dad could marry my mom again. Boy, what a mistake that would have been. I'm glad you didn't let me stop the wedding."

Getting to Know Each Other

When the boundaries about the minifamilies are no longer defining all your interactions, you begin to see the other members of your stepfamily as the unique and special individuals they are. This is another paradox of family life: As your stepfamily becomes unified, it does not swallow up each of you. Instead, it gives you each a chance to stand out and be recognized as a separate person. That character in the brown jacket is no longer "my sloppy stepson," a symbol of your husband's former marriage and the difficulties of forming a stepfamily, but Gregory, a person with whom you have a relationship. And you are no longer "Dad's friend" or even "Step-mom" but Chrissie, someone Gregory can talk to and joke with and sometimes scream at when the world is too frustrating.

Getting to know each other takes place while you are working together in the stepfamily. You and your stepsons have a great time trading elephant jokes while you dig up the garden. In the course of preparing a surprise party for your husband, you, your child, and your stepchildren discover that you can have a good time together. The party brings all of you closer.

When you know each other, your efforts to please the other members of your stepfamily are more likely to succeed. You know your stepson hates steak, so you cook his favorite, veal parmigiana, for his birthday and he is delighted. You know which flowers will let your wife know she is still the woman you were courting five years ago. Your children have picked out a special necklace for their stepmother's birthday. They know she will like it because they saw her admiring it in a store window when she took them shopping for a gift for Grandma. When the other members of the family please you, you want to be loving and generous in return. A positive cycle of caring and giving begins.

AFFECTION AND UNIFICATION

As your stepfamily becomes more unified, the family members start to feel affection for each other. The acceptance and authority stages have laid the groundwork for new closeness.

When you feel accepted by the other members of your stepfamily, you begin to open up. You lose the fear that you are constantly being judged and evaluated. You relax, fool around more, show your silly side, and begin to talk about your feelings. Every hug you give your stepchildren is not premeditated.

Your stepchildren, recognizing that you are going to be around, take the time to say hello, tell you about themselves, and show some interest in you. You become fond of each other, miss each other when the schedule keeps you apart, and feel concern when the other is having a hard time.

You can even get used to the habits that irked you when you first entered the stepfamily. For example, when Ned's son Jeff spent his first summer with his father and stepmother, Marge found that Jeff's forgetfulness drove her up a wall. She thought he was purposely leaving his things around the house so she would pick them up, forgetting his lunch so she would have to bring it to him at day camp, and forgetting his chores so she would do them for him. After a few weeks, however, she realized that he was equally forgetful when other people were involved and that he just seemed to have a harder time remembering things than other people did. She tried to teach him ways to remember and became more understanding when he forgot. The two of them became closer. One day when Ned started to yell at Jeff for forgetting to put away the baseball equipment, Marge came to his defense. Jeff was so appreciative of Marge's support that he gave her a big hug.

Living through the authority struggles also paves the way for affection. When your authority as a stepparent is not constantly being challenged by the children, you are more fun to be with and you have more fun. You can bend the rules because you know that making an exception will not threaten your power in the family. Learning that you will stand your ground gives your stepchild a greater sense of safety and security.

This security allows children to move away from constantly testing the limits and into other activities. They have more energy for growing up. As they become more mature and more respectful, they are more appealing. You may have dreaded your stepson's arrival when you knew he would spend the whole weekend disobeying you. Now that you know he'll be reasonably friendly, follow the rules most of the time, and want to share his life with you, you begin to look forward to seeing him.

Your feelings for your stepchild may never be the same as your feelings for your biological child. That is normal. Biological, legal, and historical ties do influence us. If you don't use the relationship between a biological parent and child as your measuring stick, your relationship with your stepchild can become very meaningful to both of you.

DIFFERENCES IN FAMILY DEVELOPMENT

In a nuclear family, parents assume that they will love and accept their children from birth. A problem accepting a child who is disabled or different from them is considered a failure on their part. That love for their children gives the parents the right and responsibility to discipline and guide them. Parents do a thousand and one tedious, backbreaking chores for which they are never thanked. Their reward is in seeing the child grow, develop, and express love for them.

In a stepfamily, affection, authority, and acceptance all grow with time and effort, as the table on family development shows. A stepparent often has to act like a parent before he or she loves or even accepts the stepchildren. Even if you are barely participating in your stepchildren's care, you are forced to endure their noise and their mess, wash extra dishes, buy extra food, and take them into account when you and your partner make plans.

FAMILY DEVELOPMENT

Nuclear family	*Stepfamily*
Acceptance is automatic.	Acceptance takes time.
Love and affection are immediate.	Love may never be strong; affection grows with time.
Authority comes from parental role.	Authority must be learned.
Family becomes less unified as the children grow older.	Family moves toward unification.

As a parent, you can demand good-night hugs and kisses, you get happy smiles when the children see you coming home, and you feel proud when the children's teachers or doctors tell you they are doing well. When you are a stepparent, the children may not want to kiss you or even say hello. They see you, their stepfather, as they walk in the door, and they say, "Isn't my mom here?" You cook a dinner that is not eaten; you get a bath ready and are told, "I hate baths"; you tell a bedtime story and are informed you don't tell as good stories as Mommy. You are often excluded from conferences with the children's other caretakers. You are apt to feel unappreciated.

Frieda was complaining that her three stepdaughters never thanked her for cooking for them, washing their clothes, or straightening up their room. Her friend, the biological mother of three children, said, "But children never thank their parents for those things. My kids never thank me. Your stepchildren are treating you just like a member of the family. You should be pleased. If they thanked you, it would be as if they were on their best behavior, like thanking some great-aunt."

Frieda's friend is correct; children are not in the habit of thanking their parents for routine care. However, most stepparents want to be thanked by someone. They don't feel the same gratification that parents do when their children eat, sleep, and enjoy themselves.

A good solution to this desire for appreciation is to have the biological parent do the thanking. You probably never thought of thanking your wife for making the spaghetti sauce your children like, or for driving into town to get your daughter a leotard for her gymnastics class. After all, you do those things all the time without getting a whisper of a thank you. You may be amazed at the difference a few thanks will make. Your partner will be more cheerful about helping to care for the children, and the children may even follow your example and start thanking both of you.

Nurturance and Affection

Biological parents nurture their children because they love them. Stepparents nurture their stepchildren before they love them. What happens, however, is that the acts of care that you perform, those unappreciated, endless, repetitive tasks of cooking and cleaning and reminding can lead to feelings of affection between you. You start to care about them as you care for them. When they do thank you for gluing the broken cup, ask for seconds of the dinner you made, or want *you* to take them for a haircut, you feel a sense of pride and connection. You worry when they are ill, brag about them when they win prizes, and look forward to seeing them.

Sometimes you don't realize how much you care until you miss the children. Frieda was surprised that she missed her stepdaughters when they skipped their biweekly visit:

> You know, I woke up at 7 o'clock this morning and found myself listening for their little footsteps on the stairs. When I remembered they weren't here, I didn't mind the extra sleep but I also felt a little sad. A small empty spot. I didn't think I would ever miss them after all the complaining I've done.

PROBLEM SOLVING

Your stepfamily is probably in much better shape now than it was earlier. Nonetheless, difficulties may come your way. Problems do arise in all families, and some of the problems you face in stepfamilies are complicated by the previous divorces, the children's other parents, or the schedules your children have. You still need to think strategically about solving these problems if they come up. Let's suppose, for example, your fourteen-year-old has been reported for smoking in the boys' room at school. You hear about it from his mother, who has been called by the assistant principal. You plan a meeting with your ex-wife, your son, and the principal for the next morning.

That evening you tell your wife, Teresa, what has happened. You are hoping for some warm words of comfort such as, "This could happen to anyone. Don't get too upset until you hear the whole story. If there's a problem, we'll solve it together." Instead, Teresa is angry at you for not including her in the next day's meeting and for not noticing that your son has been a little "off" lately. You are accused of being a passive father and a poor husband. You watch Teresa leave the room in a huff.

Now you feel as if you have gone back in time to that first fight-filled year you spent together. What has happened to all the good times, all the heart-to-heart talks? Your sense of despair is tripled. You just know everything is going to get worse and worse. You envision yourself walking to the courthouse for your second divorce. The rest of your life will be spent alone; you'll never trust a woman again.

Stop! Rather than letting your mind take you on this gloomy trip to nowhere, give yourself the comfort that you need. Have a little talk with yourself. Remind yourself:

- This is *not* the first year of our marriage. We have solved lots of problems together before; we'll solve this one too.
- I feel overwhelmed because I am acting like a victim. I can take control of the situation. At least I can figure out how much control is possible.

Now your mind is starting to click. If your car was making a funny noise and you stopped at a strange service station and were told that you needed a valve job, would you turn over your Master-Card and say, "Go ahead." No. The first thing you would do is get more information. You start to make a mental (or pencil-and-paper) list of the questions you would like to ask:

1. What really happened? What was he smoking? Is this the first time he has been caught? How long has my son been smoking, anyway? Whom was he with?
2. What kind of action does the school take in a case like this? Will this affect his grades? His athletic participation? What is the penalty?
3. If he was doing this knowing he could get in trouble and have all of us called in, what message is he trying to give us? Does this relate to living in two stepfamilies? Are there any changes taking place in his life I should be thinking about? Have his mother and I been communicating enough about him?
4. Is this simply a result of being fourteen? Don't most teenagers try to test the rules at some time? What do I think about his smoking? How much should his mother and I coordinate our reactions?
5. What is going on with Teresa? Did I hurt her feelings? Should she come to the meeting tomorrow also? It's her problem too.

Now you have switched roles from passive victim to active detective. You may decide to call your son and talk to him about the incident. Perhaps you should call the principal yourself and speak to him directly before the meeting. You can reopen your discussion with Teresa. You certainly cannot make the problem disappear or solve it in one evening all by yourself. You can remind yourself that this one problem will not ruin everything you have built in your family.

One trap for couples in stepfamilies is to assume that every problem is related to the divorce or the remarriage. Teachers or other professionals who are helping you can sometimes take one look at your child's record, see that the parents have two different addresses, and assume that this child has problems because he or she comes from a broken home. You must be the one who makes sure they look more carefully at your child's behavior.

If a child is showing signs of distress, there may be a problem that is related to your family situation; but the problem will most likely be connected to something that is happening currently. Is one of the parents making a change? Is a new baby on the way? Has a grandparent died recently? Is one parent's second marriage on the rocks? Children whose parents have been divorced may be especially sensitive to these changes. Rarely are they reacting to something as vague as the divorce itself, which is now several years behind them.

An exception is children who have lost a parent through death. It is possible that the children and their remaining parent have not mourned satisfactorily for the deceased parent, and some of their feelings of grief, anger, and abandonment are pushed below the surface. They come up again, usually when there is a new source of stress.

Even a child whose parents are divorced and remarried can have difficulties that are not caused by the family changes. A child can have a learning problem, react strongly to adolescence, feel left out by friends, or have a hard time getting along with a brother or sister. If you always assume the problem relates to the divorce (and is, therefore, somehow your fault), you can accumulate thousands of guilt points without helping the child at all.

Unfortunately, many people in the helping professions are not aware of the ways in which divorced or remarried families differ from the "normal," textbook nuclear family. They may interpret differences in your lifestyle as problems or miss the problems that are really there. If you feel that your family is being stereotyped by someone in a helping position, you have every right to:

1. Ask the person, quite politely, how much experience she has had with stepfamilies. Is he aware of the patterns of stepfamily life? Has she worked with children from stepfamilies before?

2. Find another professional you feel is more sympathetic, if you are not satisfied with the first person's answers.

3. Try to educate the professional. Explain very carefully your child's history and the relevant facts about your stepfamily so that you can work together to sort out the possible sources of the problem.

In any case, you and the teacher, guidance counselor, social worker, or therapist should try to work as a team. You have information and insights that can be helpful. Ultimately the problem is yours and you are going to have to solve it. The other person only gives you a little help along the way. You may as well be part of the solution from the start.

Stepparents and Schools

Many stepparents are excluded from contacts with professionals who teach, tutor, or counsel their stepchildren. Have you ever received a notice inviting parents and stepparents to a back-to-school night or graduation or school play? Does the school nurse call and use the wrong last name because she has no record of the child's parents' and stepparents' names? Does the school provide a copy of the report card for the noncustodial parent or arrange for conferences with him or her? Sometimes a small suggestion on your part can help to make school personnel aware of their oversights and lead to new policies that will help other stepparents feel more comfortable in the future.

If you feel like a parent person to your stepchild, you are entitled to attend the meeting, talk to the teachers, enjoy the play. Volunteer to teach the class first-aid techniques or go along on the field trip. You don't have to be excluded, if you don't want to be, merely because stepparents haven't been invited.

OLD AND NEW TIES

In a stepfamily, members have different kinds of ties to each other.

The Parent-Child Minifamilies

The members of each minifamily have connections with each other that they do not share with the rest of the stepfamily. They still have ties to the former nuclear family and the extended family of the former spouse. For example, when Ned's former mother-in-law died, he and his children went to the funeral. Jeff and Belinda wanted to be there, and Ned felt he could offer support to the children at their first funeral while paying his last respects to someone who had treated him generously. Marge's kids did not even consider going with the others to the funeral of an old woman they had never met. Marge thought about it and realized her presence would merely add confusion to a sad occasion. The funeral was a time when it was appropriate for the stepfamily to split into its two separate parent-child minifamilies.

You have special feelings about your children that you may not have for your stepchildren. A mother and stepmother of two teen-aged soccer players realized that when her stepson scored a goal, she was proud of him and looked at her husband to let him know that she was being a good stepmother. When her son scored a goal, she jumped up and down and hoped he would look her way to share her excitement. The connection with her son was immediate and direct; her relationship with her stepson depended on her husband as the link.

The Couple Minifamily

The couple minifamily is different from the other minifamilies because it is based on a present, rather than past, relationship. You have a life together that is private from the children. The fact that you share an intimate relationship, discuss the family finances, and have adult friends helps you give leadership to the stepfamily. If this relationship were to lose its special place, the whole stepfamily would be meaningless. People in second marriages who are not happy with each other rarely stay together "for the sake of the children."

Steprelationships

The special relationships that can develop between stepparent and stepchild or stepbrothers and stepsisters are an added bonus of living in a stepfamily. Sometimes you can help your stepchild because you have some distance from his parents and see things more clearly. You may be able to share your skills in a way that forms a special connection. Ned was pleased to teach Miriam how to program the computer she used in school. Neither of his children was interested in computers, and neither of Miriam's parents was computer literate. Marge helped Jeff be less forgetful. She worked hard and diligently, consulting both books and community experts in her efforts. Both of Jeff's biological parents had always accepted his forgetfulness as part of his personality; they couldn't imagine trying to change it.

Katie (of the family with secret agendas in Chapter Five) was delighted when Erica, her older stepsister, finally began to pay some attention to her. Erica, who was an honor roll student in college, was able to talk Katie into trying harder at school because Katie looked up to her so much. Erica succeeded in helping Katie become interested in school and live up to her potential, where two parents, two stepparents, and many teachers had failed.

One stepfather opened up emotionally to his two-year-old stepson more than he ever had with his own children, who were now in their teens:

> I feel sad when I realize what I missed with my own kids. I never knew what fun they could be. I was working all the time when they were this young, and I was in a terrible marriage. They lost out. I feel guilty about them, but I'm not going to let that stop me from loving Petie the way I do. I learn something from him every day, and I'm learning more about what a father can be.

The Stepfamily

The stepfamily is the basic family with whom you live. You work together to get things done; you share the ups and downs of your daily lives. The hard times you have been through as a stepfamily hold you together the way that "blood ties" do in the nuclear family.

LOVE

If you love your stepchildren and they love you and you all know it, you can skip this section. Love becomes a problem in stepfamilies only when you are looking for it and think you can't find it. For example:

- You think you should feel instant, automatic, consistent, strong love for your stepchildren and are berating yourself because you don't.
- Your spouse is berating you because he or she thinks you do not have the right kind or right amount of love for your stepchildren.
- You are disappointed because your stepchildren do not seem to love you.
- You are heartbroken because your spouse and your children do not love each other the way you would like them to.

If one of these love problems is familiar to you, it's time to separate the myth from the reality. The reality of the stepfamily is this:

- You are not required to love your stepchild.
- Your stepchild is not required to love you.
- No one can force you to love a stepchild or a stepchild to love you.
- The love you do develop for your stepchild may come slowly or suddenly, if and when it comes.
- You can have a great stepfamily without the kind of love you think you do not have.

Love has many forms and many meanings. In a nuclear family, love is unconditional and immediate. In a stepfamily, love grows from acceptance, authority, and affection. Sometimes your love for your husband spills over onto his children. Love is expressed through your acts of caring.

Sometimes the feelings of love you do have are confusing. A five-year-old girl asked her stepmother, "I love you so much. Is that okay?" You may confuse the loving feelings between you and a stepchild with feelings of sexual attraction and be embarrassed to feel this way about someone in your family. This love does not feel safe. Actually the love is safe and the sexual feelings are normal, but acting them out is unhealthy and illegal.

The relationship you have as a stepparent starts with the awareness of the differences between you and your stepchild. The loving feelings you have develop despite these differences. You know your relationship is not one of duty: The child doesn't love you because of an accident of birth or because you have the same name, and your love for your stepchild cannot be possessive because you have never owned him. You have a head start on the biological parent in seeing your stepchild as an individual because you don't have as big a stake in the way he or she turns out.

The lack of biological connection also makes you more vulnerable. Your stepchildren can hurt you deeply if you love them and they push you away. If your second marriage ends in divorce, you may never see them again. One stepfather, whose own children lived in Europe with their mother and grandparents, found himself holding back from his three-year-old stepdaughter:

> I am so afraid of losing another child that I just can't let out the love I know I feel for her. I think I stick to a more disciplinary role because I don't want to be heartbroken every time she leaves for her dad's house. What if she grows up and doesn't like me because I'm her stepfather? I don't know if I could take it.

Unfortunately, this stepfather doesn't realize that a child this young can grow up accepting and loving both a father and a stepfather. The label of "stepfather," when she learns what it means, will not estrange her from someone she has known most of her life.

Love in your stepfamily can be a new experience. You realize that love is not a limited resource. The love you give to your stepchildren is not taken away from your children. You learn that you can love people who make you angry. You can love your stepchildren and nonetheless feel relieved when they are gone for the weekend and the house quiets down.

Once your stepfamily has become unified and you share your affection or love for one another, you may stop thinking of yourselves as a stepfamily. You don't introduce your husband as your "second husband" or your cat as your "third cat." When you are in the affection stage, you start to think of your stepfamily simply as your family.

CHAPTER EIGHT
The Remarried Couple

*I*t's one of those days. Everything is going wrong. You're home waiting for the plumber because your hot water heater is flooding the basement. You discover that your stepson has been using the notes for your presentation to the board of directors to make paper airplanes. Your husband is meeting with his ex-wife, who wants him to double her child support payments because you have received a promotion. You decide to do your nails while you're waiting and find that your stepdaughter has left the cover off your best nail polish. It's now as hard as a rock. Is it any wonder you are asking yourself, "How did I get into this?"

It's simple. You fell in love. You found someone you could get along with. You felt special together; you still do. You wanted what most people want—to live your life as part of a couple. The stepchildren and the ex-spouse were not what you bargained for, but you were willing to put up with them in order to marry the man of your choice.

THE COUPLE MINIFAMILY

Your couple minifamily is at the center of your stepfamily. The relationship you have with your spouse is the reason for the stepfamily's existence in the first place. You have a huge responsibility for keeping the stepfamily together and yet, compared to most married couples, you've hardly had a chance to get acquainted.

Being in a second marriage is different from being in a first marriage in several significant ways:

1. One or both of you have been divorced.
2. One or both of you have children from your first marriage.
3. One or both of you have a former spouse.
4. You are older, and the difference in your ages may be greater than in your first marriage.

If you have never been married before but are now married to someone who is divorced, these factors also affect you.

Couple relationships have a life of their own, in addition to each of your individual lives. People in first marriages go through a series of stages in their relationships. In a second marriage you face several stages at once. For example, you are going through a very exclusive, "eyes-only-for-you" stage and a child-rearing stage at the same time. Add to this a mid-life crisis, aging parents, or a major job decision, and your life seems as simple as a Russian novel. Luckily, your maturity and experience can help you to cope with these stresses.

RESULTS OF HAVING BEEN DIVORCED

Intimacy was often missing from the marriages that failed. In your second marriage, you are looking for someone with whom more closeness will be possible.

Intimacy

You may be more capable of being intimate now. A divorce forces you to face yourself. Many people talk about their feelings for the first time when the marriage is breaking up. They go to support groups or therapy; they talk to their friends more openly. Sometimes people even approach their parents with more honesty and openness. If you and your partner meet while you are both going through similar divorce experiences, your mutual sympathy may bring you close to each other. You each know in your gut what the other is feeling.

Some divorced parents have learned to be intimate from their children. As you take care of children without your partner's help, you discover that you can nurture and love them. You are capable of sharing their hurts and their joys.

The divorce can also make you wary of new relationships. Do you want to make yourself vulnerable again? The first time you did not know how much a marriage could change you, how much pain could result from what you thought was everlasting love. Now you know better. Shouldn't you protect yourself? What if you do fall in love again and discover it is no good? What if you have to end another relationship? Could you live with the guilt of leaving again?

Doubts like these are very common after a divorce, but most people put them aside as they start to heal. Although two-thirds of the recently divorced people interviewed in a study done in Central Pennsylvania said they were not interested in remarriage, two and a half years later nearly one-third of them were already remarried.[1] Eventually four-fifths of the divorced men and three-quarters of the divorced women in this country remarry.[2] The desire for closeness and belonging outweighs the fears of making the same mistakes or being hurt again.

Goals

Many people get married the first time not knowing what to expect and what to aim for in a marriage. The goals that you have for your second marriage are probably clearer. You are likely to care less about moonlight and flowers and more about communication and cooperation. You know that marriage is not just romance; it is living together on a daily, monthly, and yearly basis. You want to share your perspective on life, and you want to share more with your partner.

Openness and honesty are two qualities people seek in their second marriages. You are determined to share your feelings, tell your partner what you want, express your anger, and do everything you can to keep this relationship on the path to success.

There are also times when honesty may hurt your partner. How can you tell him truthfully that you don't want to stay in a certain motel because you and your first husband used to go there? Do you want her to know you are depressed because today would be your twentieth anniversary if you were still married and because your ex-wife called you to remind you? Do you dare to tell him, honestly, how spoiled his kids are?

Your desire to be honest would lead you to tell the truth. Your delicacy and tact might lead you to withhold parts of it. This is one dilemma of your second marriage. In wrestling with it in your own way, you will make what seems like the best decision at the time. Most people discover that no one rule fits every occasion. If you find that you should have said more or could have said less, you remember that the next time the question comes up. You learn to understand yourself and your relationship better.

Holding On to the First Marriage

Ending your first marriage, as we have seen, is not something that happens once and for all. Some people, even those who are physically separated or legally divorced, are still ending the first marriage when they start a new relationship.

Rick and Rosalyn described this kind of experience: "We're in love. We're right for each other. We just met too soon." It was too soon because Rick, who had been separated from his wife Anne for only six months when he met Rosalyn, was still emotionally attached to his marriage. He treated Anne more like a wife than a coparent. He chatted with her every evening when he called to say good night to his sons. He helped her out when she had problems in arranging child care. He asked her to help him on his taxes. He even took her out to dinner on her birthday because he didn't want her to celebrate alone.

The relationship with Rosalyn helped Rick see what had been missing in his marriage. Rosalyn was open and warm. He could talk to her about his feelings more than he ever had with Anne. As a couple, Rosalyn and Rick became close emotionally, intellectually, and sexually. When they had disagreements, they could listen to each other's point of view without blowing up or storming out.

Whenever Rick's lingering attachment to Anne came to the surface, Rosalyn would become angry and upset. One day Rosalyn and Rick went to a flea market; he bought a pitcher for Anne because it matched some dishes she had from her grandmother. Rosalyn was very jealous. On another occasion she and Rick had dinner to celebrate the six-month anniversary of the day they had met, and Rick told her the story of his honeymoon with Anne.

Rosalyn lost patience. How could Rick even be thinking about his past when they got along so well? She lost all her sympathy for his pain about the divorce. If he wanted to be sad, he could go off somewhere and talk to someone else. She was not going to listen to stories about how much Rick had loved another woman.

Rick was a member of three different minifamilies—his couple relationship with his first wife, his couple relationship with Rosalyn, and his visiting-parent minifamily with his children. From our spectator position, we see these conflicting loyalties clearly. But Rick didn't think of them as minifamilies. His mind didn't store his thoughts about the past with Anne and his conversations in the present with Rosalyn in different compartments.

Rosalyn belonged to only one minifamily, the couple relationship with Rick. When Rick brought Anne, in name or thought, across the boundary of this minifamily, she felt resentful. Sometimes Rosalyn wished she had met Rick two years in the future, with the first marriage completely behind him. By then, however, she thought he might have found someone else.

There was also a positive side to the freshness of the divorce experience in Rick's life. The pain of his separation opened him up to more intimacy than he had ever known before. He was more vulnerable, more aware of his feelings, and more willing to change his attitudes and habits. These were qualities that Rosalyn appreciated.

Rick's split loyalties between the two minifamilies provoked Rosalyn's jealousy. She felt she had to guard the new relationship or Rick might just let it slip away. She could not understand why Rick did not seem to act on his own behalf in focusing his attention on their relationship and pushing his ex-wife away.

It was not Anne herself who got between them; she wanted the divorce. It was the difference between Rick and Rosalyn about how Rick should treat Anne. Rosalyn's pressure on Rick to make the minifamily boundaries clearer pushed him to let go of Anne. He ended the nightly chats, said no to her baby-sitting requests, and stopped buying her presents. However, starting a new relationship before this change had taken place caused difficulties for the new couple.

THE CHILDREN AND THE NEW RELATIONSHIP

Love, we have been told, is not a resource that is limited. There's more than enough to go around for everyone. But time, energy, laps, front seats in the car, and hands to hold are finite. Have you ever tried hugging a man who has two children on his lap?

Children quite literally get in the way of your new relationship and can continue to come between you after you are married. The romance quickly goes out of a day in the woods when you bring the children along. McDonald's is not quite the atmosphere for intimacy. Children edge their way in between you as you talk or even as you lie in bed together in the morning.

People in love for the first time can stay up all night without being tired. They can stop eating and not feel hungry. They barely notice the rain or snow as they walk along holding hands. Although most couples do not remain in this state of intoxication for long, they are enriched later on by memories of the "crazy times" when they drove to the lake at midnight, ran up outragious long-distance phone bills talking to each other, or stayed together in hotel rooms for entire weekends. Retelling their history rekindles the sense of excitement they shared.

Caring for children definitely limits spontaneity. You can't dash out of the house at midnight and leave a child sleeping in her bed. You can't simply stare at each other and giggle throughout breakfast if your kids are throwing pancakes. If you want to get away without the children, you are dependent on the other parent, baby-sitters, or relatives. At the last minute child-care arrangements can dissolve or a child can become ill. You may get your weekend away but have to spend half of it waiting while your partner calls his former spouse on the phone to find out about his daughter's temperature.

Sometimes both of you feel that the children are interfering with your relationship. At other times you and your spouse may disagree about whether the children are getting in the way. Rosalyn, who loved flea markets, convinced Rick and his children to visit one with her. She wanted to enjoy herself with Rick as she had the last time (at least until he bought the pitcher for Anne). They had walked around slowly, sharing their reactions to the things they saw, talking to the people displaying the merchandise, holding hands, and making up fantasies about their future together.

The day with the children was completely different for Rosalyn: "We walked through the flea market. Rick was up ahead with three kids all over his arms. I was trailing behind looking at things that interested me. For me, that was not going to a flea market with Rick."

Rick's experience of the same day was not disappointing: "I loved having Rosalyn there. I couldn't hold her hand, but it meant a lot to me to have her there with me and my kids. I loved just looking back at her and seeing her looking over the things she liked. It definitely made me feel closer to her."

Their different perceptions came from belonging to different minifamilies. Rosalyn's allegiance was to her minifamily with Rick; Rick was loyal to his couple and his parent-child minifamilies. He felt good when both minifamilies were in the same place at the same time. The good feeling inside of him compensated for the extra space that the children put between him and Rosalyn.

However, even Rick could reach the point of feeling annoyed that his children were interfering with his couple relationship. At that point he would tell them all to watch TV and not bother him. He would go into the bedroom with Rosalyn and close the door.

Time with Children

The simplest way in which the children impinge on the couple's relationship is by absorbing the time of the parent and/or the step-parent. We have already described how stepfamilies are organized around the times when children come and go on their visits. Five-sixths of the children with divorced parents see their visiting parent less than one day a week over the course of the year.[3] In a recent study, 60 percent of the children had not seen the visiting parent once during the previous year.[4] Although the stepfamilies of these children do not have to cope with the complexities of scheduling parental visits, they do have full-time responsibility for the children.

Your children not only spend some time alone with you; they also share a lot of the time you have together as a couple. They need to be taken to doctors' appointments, extracurricular activities, barbers, and shoe stores. You must make arrangements over the phone with the dentist, the car pool, and the friend who is coming for the weekend. Their care also involves extra shopping, cooking, and cleaning. Even children who merely visit usually do so on weekends, the time a couple would ordinarily have to relax together.

As a parent, you take all this for granted. As a stepparent without children, you are astonished at how much busier your life is now. When you talk with your newly married friends who do not have stepchildren, they seem to be free and easy in comparison.

If both partners have children who are with them frequently, there is some reciprocity. You can take all of the children, yours and his, on a special outing at the same time. If your husband is taking his son to visit a cousin you have no desire to see, you can use the free time to play computer games with your son or buy him some new clothes for school. You are not at home alone, feeling excluded.

The time taken up with child care seems to cause the most difficulties when one member of the couple has no children or has children who rarely visit. The partner without children feels as if he or she is in competition with the children for the parent's attention.

When Thursday's paper arrived, with the big entertainment section of the week, Alice would look first under Children's Events to see where she could take her daughter that weekend. Her husband, Frank, would turn to the Nightlife section to find places to take Alice. When it was time for Frank and Alice to spend an evening out together, Alice would never have any ideas about where she wanted to go. She would leave it up to Frank to do the research. Frank finally got angry. He knew Alice could make plans for her daughter. Why couldn't she make plans for him, too? He resented all her planning energy going into one of her minifamilies and none into the other.

Frank also protested when Alice's daughter, Elizabeth, who was ten, invited her friends to sleep over on the weekend. He didn't like having "silly" girls stay up late and make noise. Sometimes they slept on the living-room floor, and he and Alice had to spend the evening watching TV in their bedroom. He did not understand why Alice usually gave in when Elizabeth asked permission for a sleepover party.

The disagreements between Frank and Alice over Elizabeth were a result of the different perspectives each had as a member of one or two minifamilies. If Elizabeth had been Frank's child, he might have been in the habit of looking at the Children's Events section and leaving the Nightlife to Alice. He might easily have been the one to grant permission for the sleepovers despite Alice's disapproval.

Benefits

One benefit of having children from a first marriage is that you see each other as parents and potential parents. Maybe you are especially warm and charming when you're with your kids, and you like your partner to see you this way. If you are not a parent, you get a preview of what your new partner will be like if you have children together. You may find it important to know that you are marrying someone who can be a loving parent.

Parents feel good when other adults like their children. When you see your new wife playing with your kids and obviously liking them, you get a warm feeling in your heart. Tell her about it.

You and your partner can also have fun with the children: at children's movies, amusements parks, Disneyworld, fairs, and zoos. Although you could go to some of these places as two adults, you probably would not enjoy them as much.

The children are a project the two of you share, at least for the time they are in your home. You may enjoy planning outings together, preparing meals, fixing up their rooms, or complimenting each other on the good job each of you did. Working together as a parenting and problem-solving team gives you another way to get to know each other. Caring for the children gives you a chance to work out some of your differences. It may be too much, too fast, but it does provide an opportunity for compromise, discussion, and learning.

The children can bring both of you joy and pride when they are loving toward you or growing up in the ways you want them to. Regardless of who originally produced them, they reflect the good job you two are doing as a team.

PROBLEM SOLVING

Let's suppose you have never had children of your own and you are married to a man with two children. Although your situation is a common type of remarriage, it is novel for you. Your experience may be confusing and upsetting. Whenever you try to stick up for yourself or criticize the children, you feel as if you are being pushed into the role of the wicked stepmother. If you try to make some changes, will your marriage go down the drain?

First, let's look carefully at your complaints. Here is an imaginary list:

1. When the children are here (every weekend), we never go out as a couple. We haven't been to a movie or dinner without the kids in months. We haven't been dancing since my cousin's wedding last July.
2. We have no privacy. His kids are always butting their way into our business.
3. The children borrow anything they like without asking, often things that are expensive or things I need for work.
4. When I say no to the children, my husband does not support me.
5. When I criticize the children to my husband, he thinks I am being selfish and do not understand kids.
6. The children don't keep in touch with us. They arrive Friday night and want to be driven somewhere Saturday morning. They never call during the week to arrange for rides or make plans.
7. When the children leave on Sunday, my husband is so exhausted from knocking himself out with them that all he wants to do is read the paper.

Your list does not indicate that you are basically unhappy with your marriage. You probably love and respect your husband. The problems revolve around a lack of privacy as a couple and the role that his children play in your marriage. Your strategy for change should begin with the relationship between the parent-child minifamily and the couple minifamily.

You need to choose a goal to work on. One of these might do:

Goal A: Arranging more time to be alone together as a couple

Goal B: Joining together to set more limits for the children

Goal C: Understanding each other's viewpoints

Any one of these could be a reasonable beginning. Goal A is probably the best choice because when you feel closer as a couple, you will be in better frames of mind for goal B, working together to set limits, and goal C, understanding each other. Goal B is not a good starting point unless your husband has already agreed that more limits are needed. You may have some convincing to do first. As you plan for goal A, he may see that setting limits is in order.

As the first step, find a time to be together. Your husband suggests going out during the week when the children are not around. You could start with this. Even if both of you are at home most evenings, you may be in different worlds. He's painting the basement stairs, and you're writing thank-you notes for your Christmas gifts. By the time you've finished, he has painted the steps and is soaking in the tub. He comes out and turns on a hockey game. You fold the clothes and pay some bills. Before you know it, you're both ready for bed. You've hardly been in the same room for ten minutes at a stretch. The weekend is coming and you won't have any time together then.

Going out on week nights has advantages: Places are less crowded and less expensive. Some couples find that setting aside an evening each week when they make no other plans helps them to be close to each other. If you don't go out, you can be sure to eat dinner together, talk to each other about something that is on your mind, or watch a special movie together on TV.

Let's suppose a week night is not going to work. You work ten hours, four days a week, and have Fridays off. Your husband goes to bed early and gets up at 5:30 to jog. From Monday through Thursday you barely say hello to each other. Your need to connect is even greater. So you are left with the weekends. You can:

- Change the schedule so the children arrive Saturday afternoon instead of Friday night. Then you would have Friday nights together.

- Change the schedule so you have one or two weekends a month without the children or with the children coming for only part of the weekend.
- Leave the children with a baby-sitter. This means finding local baby-sitters, deciding which of you is responsible for making the arrangements, paying for your time alone, and overruling the children's objections to being left with other people.

Choosing any one of these options is apt to bring up other issues. That's a good thing. Changing the schedule forces your husband and his ex-wife to revise their expectations of each other. If this is more than he is willing to try for now, you can work on finding baby-sitters. Your husband says that you can't afford to pay for a baby-sitter, but the underlying problem, you learn from your discussion, is that your husband feels so guilty about his divorce (which occurred four years ago) that he can't bear to leave the children with a substitute caretaker. If these are his feelings, he needs to do a lot of talking and a lot of looking around at what other fathers do in similar situations. He is already seeing his children more frequently than 85 percent of the divorced fathers in this country. If you can really uncover feelings like these, you have hit the jackpot in increasing your communication as a couple and your understanding of each other.

You can listen to your husband, praise his concern for his children, and reassure him that getting a baby-sitter from time to time may even have some advantages for his daughters. Taking you out alone will be giving them the model of a couple who care for each other as well as for the children. The girls can become more independent of him. If you find a good baby-sitter, the children may even look forward to her arrival. She will let them stay up late, make them popcorn, or tell them amazing stories. She may even introduce them to some other children their own age in your neighborhood.

After you have heard him out, you can ask him to consider your frustrations. You married him because you love him, not his children. You want to make him happy. You want to be proud of him when he takes you out. You want to talk to him about serious things. You want to enjoy yourselves with other people. Be firm about your specific demands. You are not asking him to leave his girls; you are asking him to be a good husband. Focus on what you want from him as your husband, not on how hard it is to have the children around. In this way you keep the discussion within the couple minifamily and do not cross the boundary into his territory of the parent-child minifamily.

Now, if all of this talking has succeeded, you have cleared the time to go out together. You still have to decide where to go and how much money you can afford if you do go out. Will you invite another couple to join you or go by yourselves? You can enjoy making these decisions together.

This seems like a lot of work just to do something that most newlyweds do easily and naturally: get out of the house together for some fun. But look at all you have accomplished:

1. You have had some good talks and shared one of the underlying reasons why you have not been going out.

2. You have recognized your differences in attitude about leaving the children with a sitter or changing the child-care schedule. These differences result from your loyalty to different minifamilies.

3. You have strengthened your couple minifamily merely by making a commitment to set aside time for each other.

4. If you chose the baby-sitter alternative, you have begun to set some new limits for the children, to expand your resources for caring for the children, and to challenge your husband's assumptions about what being a good father means.

5. If you chose the alternative of changing the schedule, and succeeded, you have made your husband's divorce agreement more flexible.

Your strategy could also reveal some other information about your relationship. Suppose your husband brings up a series of reasons why he cannot spend the time with you, and you counter them. He says there are no baby-sitters in the neighborhood, and you mention the teenage daughter of a mutual friend nearby. He says he has yard work to do, and you remind him that he cannot do that at night. Finally, he comes out with the real reason. Maybe when the two of you go out and other men look at you, he feels jealous and would rather stay safely at home together. Maybe he's very nervous about finances right now because he's facing a potential lawsuit at work. Maybe he's angry because he thinks your sex life could be better. Whatever his reason may be, you are better off knowing what it is and facing it directly instead of using the children's presence as an excuse to avoid a real issue between you or a real concern that one of you feels.

The Right Fight

Remarried couples are often in danger of picking fights over the children in order to avoid the fights that are brewing between the couple as people. Underneath your disagreements about children knocking on your door when they are scared at night may lurk a problem about your sex life. Behind the argument about your sloppy kids may be the argument about sloppy you.

Using a disagreement about the children as a shield between the two of you is not good for them or for your relationship. Not bringing your fights out into the open, with words, can erode your marriage. Making the children the villains can cause them to feel guilty and will also cause one of you to feel very resentful about their presence.

Here is one way to tell whether the hurt, disappointment, or anger that you associate with the children has some other real cause. Ask yourself, "Would this same behavior always make me so angry?" Maybe your stepson did spill his milk right after you washed the kitchen floor. It's not the first time. Why are you in a rage today, when you usually mop it up and forget it? Are you angry at your wife, your brother, or your boss? If you can get to the real source of the anger, you may be able to do something about whatever made you mad in the first place.

RELATIONSHIP WITH THE FORMER SPOUSE

Your former spouse and/or your partner's former spouse also intrude into your couple relationship. His presence at transition time, or her voice on the phone, can be a concrete interruption in the flow of your everyday life. The children may seem to bring their other parent with them when they visit or return from a visit. Their appearance or attitudes may remind you of the other parent. Sometimes you think they are arguing the former spouse's cause in your home or lobbying for what is best for him or her. One teenager, for example, turned down her father's offer to pay for boarding school primarily because she knew her mother would lose her child support payments if she went away to school.

Even if there were no children in the first marriage, or you have barely any contact with your former spouse, he or she may seem to be hovering around as a ghost, reminding you of past mistakes or tempting you to make comparisons between your first and second marriages. The former spouse also interferes with your image of a marriage: You don't want to be number two; you want to be number one.

The former spouse has often had several roles in your life. You originally married that person because you were in love or thought you were. You may still have some fond memories of your romance, your courtship, or parts of your married life. He or she then became your divorced spouse. You went through a period of disillusionment, hurt, and anger. You may still feel some anger and resentment toward your ex-spouse. Nevertheless, he or she is the other parent of your children. As parents, you communicate with each other and recognize each other's importance in the children's lives. You may also respect each other and treat each other civilly.

What often happens is that you and your current partner are seeing your former spouse in two different roles at the same time. Rosalyn, for example, tried to accept Rick's cordial relationship with his ex-wife, Anne, because it helped him to maintain a relationship with his children. When Rick bought Anne the pitcher, however, he was thinking of the Anne he had married and loved; he was not buying a pitcher for the mother of his children.

Seeing that Rick still had some fond feelings for Anne made Rosalyn jealous. Her mind told her that Rick was, after all, getting a divorce and that he was happy with her. Rationally, she did not fear that he would resume his former marriage. Still, she did not like the little corner of Rick's heart in which Anne still seemed to dwell. She wanted all of his love.

Usually when your spouse talks of his former spouse, you hear lots of criticism and bitterness. You develop the picture of a devilish creature who is eager to devour the children and make paupers of your husband and you. One day, however, you find your husband very considerately arranging to drive her to the airport when she's taking his children on a trip to see her parents. You are flabbergasted that he wants to do her a favor and begin to doubt everything he has said about her. Maybe he still loves her, after all. Now you are jealous and angry at him.

Most human relationships are complex and contradictory. We get angry at the people we love. We hurt our closest family members. One day we are praising each other, and the next cutting each other to bits. The human heart can contain a greater variety of feelings than we think possible. Being on the sidelines of your partner's relationship with an ex-husband or ex-wife, you see a flat picture of that relationship rather than a three-dimensional model with all its ambivalence.

Your partner knows you want to be number one. She shares with you the negative feelings she has toward her former husband to reassure you of your spot in her heart, and these are the feelings you want to hear about. Then, when you are given a more rounded view, when you glimpse another part of the relationship, you are shocked and may feel deceived.

Competing Minifamilies

If you have been divorced and are now remarried, you are a member of two couple minifamilies. Although the couple of the first marriage is no longer a sexual and intimate relationship, you may have loyalties to your first partner. You may think your ex-wife is a terrific mother and respect her advice in caring for the children. Once you have worked through your divorce experience, you may be able to chat with her in a friendly way without feeling angry or threatened. Your new spouse, however, is likely to misinterpret your friendliness as a desire to return to your first wife. You are likely to arouse her jealously in ways you would never imagine. For example:

- Frank went to pick up Elizabeth, his stepdaughter, at her father's house one afternoon. On his way to the bathroom there, he noticed, on her father's bed, a blanket that matched the blanket he and his wife, Alice, had on their bed. He couldn't believe he and Alice had been sleeping under the same cover that Alice had slept under with her first husband.

• Patricia often knew when her husband was talking to his ex-wife on the phone because he used a special sweet voice. He talked to her so softly and tenderly that Patricia would find herself feeling jealous and wishing he would hang up. It did not matter that he also used his sweet voice when he spoke to his mother, his mother-in-law, and his secretary.

• Rosalyn felt that her relationship with Rick, even after they were married, would not be as important as his former relationship with Anne unless they had a child together. She knew that a marriage could end, and she had seen that ties established through having children can last a lifetime. Although she was now Rick's wife, she felt jealous because he had the strong and permanent ties of parenthood with another woman.

• Ned felt jealous when Marge sat next to Robbie's dad at Robbie's swim meet and then went out to lunch with Robbie and his dad, her former husband.

• Carol understood that her husband, Len, met with his first wife each month to talk about the children, scheduling, and finances. She knew that he viewed these as business meetings. But she was eaten up with jealousy because the meetings took place in his former wife's home, which was also his old home. She felt that he would be pulled right back into his old role there. When Len agreed to meet with his ex-wife at the nearby Howard Johnson's, Carol was greatly relieved.

• Ned was telling his daughter Belinda a story about how he gave her a bottle in the middle of the night when she was a baby. He said, "I always got up with you at 4 a.m. because your mother was such a heavy sleeper." Marge felt a pang of jealously at being reminded that Ned used to sleep with somebody else.

You may not realize you are being loyal to your former couple minifamily in putting up with treatment you don't like from your former spouse. Helen's ex-husband was very often late in sending the child support payments to which he had agreed. Helen needed the money to support herself and her daughter Katie. She and Will had taken on the burden of a big house so that each child could have a private bedroom. Their money situation was tight. Helen never let Will know how angry and worried she became when her check was late. Will would be incensed and would call Helen's ex-husband names, but Helen would be quiet and seem to defend him. That was her way of not betraying him. She had fronted for him with bill collectors many times in her first marriage and was used to this role and to his irresponsibility with money.

One day, for no particular reason, Helen reached her limit. Her monthly check was ten days late, so she called her lawyer and she also called her ex-husband's boss. She was fit to be tied. Will couldn't believe that she had been angry all along. When they shared their feelings, they were able to work out a strategy for making more demands on her ex-husband and for arranging their finances to provide a cushion in case the money was late. When Helen stepped out of the role she had assumed in the first marriage, of protecting her husband's behavior in regard to money, she was able to feel closer to her second husband even before any of the money problems were actually cleared up.

As Helen and Will started to talk about the money issues, they realized that they had never checked out each other's assumptions about money and how it was to be shared between them. Facing their differences about finances and working them out required a lot of talking, a little bit of arguing, and the courage to acknowledge that differences existed. Blaming Helen's ex-husband for their money problems had prevented them from understanding each other better.

Close Encounters with the Former Spouse

A second wife dreads being confused with the husband's first wife. If your husband's first wife uses his last name and you, his second wife, also use his last name, you are both Mrs. Joe Hubbard. If you live in the same town, you may get each other's mail or phone calls. Your husband's ex-wife calls him at work and says, "This is Mrs. Hubbard." The switchboard puts her right through. You call him at work, and the operator says, "Oh, yes, you called a little while ago." You are not unusual if you feel she is pretending that she's still married to him.

Couples who live close to their former spouses run into them unexpectedly in public. You might enter a restaurant and have to face your wife's former husband seated there with a date. One formerly married couple had gone to college together. When their twenty-fifth reunion came, they both attended, each with a new spouse. They felt so uncomfortable about being there together that they made sure not to be present at the same events.

Decision Making

When you and your partner want to make certain kinds of decisions about your lives, you must consult your former spouses. You have less freedom to direct the course of your lives than most couples in first marriages. You two must develop especially good communication to keep from having every decision you make hinge on how it will affect one set of children or a former spouse.

AGE DIFFERENCES

The average ages at which men and women in the United States get married are as follows:[5]

	Men	*Women*
First marriage	24	22
Second marriage	35	32

Even if you have not previously been married and divorced, being older when you get married affects your relationship. You are more definite about your likes and dislikes. If you have been living alone, you are not used to sharing decisions about your daily life with someone else. He thinks you should move into his house because he has more space and his children are used to the neighborhood. But you have just fixed up your condo to suit you and you're not sure you want to give that up. What about the Early

American furniture you've been stripping and refinishing? There's no place for that in his house.

Being older might mean you are in a more advanced and responsible career position. Moving to another city would be out of the question. You are used to meeting the expectations of your company. Will you still be able to get work done at night when her children are around? What about the breakfast meetings you used to have in your apartment? You can't easily move them to your new stepfamily home.

Sometimes divorcing individuals make career changes or return to school. Maybe you have just made a commitment to repaying thousands of dollars in student loans. Maybe you feel you must work harder to establish yourself in a new field just when your new spouse wants you around for socializing and helping with the children. When your children are home, you want to be a parent, and when they go off, you want the freedom to turn into a workaholic.

Attention has been focused recently on the special difficulties of the dual-career family. The stepfamily can seem like still another career added on. You may be a remarried, dual-parent, dual-career, dual-life-cycle-stage family. When you're overwhelmed and flat on your back from the complexity of it all, it's a comfort to know what hit you.

Being older probably means that you have more responsibility for your parents. You may send them money or help them once a week with the grocery shopping. When you go away on vacation, you have to arrange for someone to check in with your mother while you're gone. You may have to find a nursing home for a parent or make some difficult decisions about his or her ability to live alone. The time needed for these responsibilities can interfere with your marriage. Moreover, the stress that you may be under in coping with an ill parent puts a strain on both of you. It can also open up another area of disagreement between the two of you about the best course of action or how involved you should be.

Partners in a second marriage, on the average, have greater differences in ages. You may each be dealing with a different stage of the life cycle. Phil had a son entering college and his new wife, Dianne, had a son entering first grade. Phil was interested in clearing his schedule for more travel, and she wanted to be more involved with the community. She wanted to have another child; he did not. Rosa was a successful college professor when she married

Clark, who was ten years younger than she and just starting out in business for himself. She wanted to invest their money safely for retirement; he wanted to take risks with it to build his business.

Talking together about these differences, just as you talk about your differences in child rearing or expectations for marriage, is the best thing you can do to keep your marriage solid. Differences, in themselves, do not destroy marriages; but differences that are unrecognized are easily misinterpreted. The resulting mistrust and poor communication can ruin your marriage.

Clark, for example, thought Rosa's hesitation in putting money into his business meant that she no confidence in his ability. It was only when he heard her talking with a colleague of her own age that he realized her behavior might have more to do with her career than his.

GETTING CLOSE AND STAYING CLOSE

Your second marriage is definitely not the same as your first marriage or a typical first marriage. On the negative side, these differences can mean that:

You fear another failure

You have less privacy than in a first marriage

Your finances are strained

You have to cope with problems with the children

Your life is overloaded with responsibilities

You have different perspectives coming from different minifamilies

Your age differences give you different priorities

You have more disagreements

On the positive side, these differences can mean that:

You are more mature

You know yourselves better

Your expectations are more flexible and realistic

You have made a better choice of marriage partner

You care about working out your differences

You have more resources available

You can rely on each other for help

Your differences can enrich your life together and make it exciting

You know more about forming close relationships

WAYS TO KEEP YOUR MARRIAGE TOGETHER

The primary reason most remarried people give for their greater happiness in the second marriage is having found and married the right person. When you feel this way about your current spouse, it is much easier to put up with the distractions and differences that come along with your stepfamily.

Your first partner may have been chosen because your parents liked him or your parents hated him. Ned often told Marge that if he had met her twenty years before, when she was first married, she wouldn't have given him the time of day. He was a long-haired, unshaven hippie, and she was working as a model. The experience of growing up helps you to make a choice that is good for you. The second time, people know both single life and married life and usually get married because they want to share their lives with the person they are choosing.

Communication

Something as simple as talking to each other can be a lifesaver for your marriage. Talking is not just saying your piece but also listening to the other person. One couple scheduled a time each week to talk about any problems that had come up. Another couple said they would sometimes wake up in the middle of the night to talk: "When we've been so busy that we hardly see each other, we miss each other. Sometimes I get up at 4 a.m. and look over at Michael and he's awake too. Then we'll talk until 5 or 6 in the morning."

The magical part of talking and listening to each other is that problems you know cannot easily be solved are much easier to live with if you share them.

Don't forget to talk about topics other than your problems. If you cannot remember the last time you told your partner that you love her, that you are glad you married him, that you are proud of her, or that you think he's good-looking, do it tonight. Don't be like the couple who went to a marriage counselor because divorce looked imminent:

SHE: He never tells me that he loves me.

HE: That's not true. I told you when I married you, in 1975. If I change my mind, I'll tell you. If not, why do I have to tell you again?

Privacy

In your second marriage you often have to make a conscious effort to find time and space to be alone. You need to think about babysitters and getting away without the children. One couple did not want to entertain all the visitors who dropped by to see them at their beach house because their time to be alone, without the children, was so limited. They told their friends and relatives to come by invitation only.

Many remarried couples argue about closing doors in their homes. The parent is used to an open-door policy for the children, and the stepparent is not. Using closed doors as a signal to the children that they are to disturb you only if there is an emergency can be helpful in finding some privacy.

Shared Values

Working toward shared values gives you a sense of closeness. You may have chosen your second mate because the two of you agree about what is important.

One couple prided themselves on their healthy habits. They served only vegetarian food and went jogging regularly as a family of six. Supporting each other's parenting and trying to reverse the habits the children had learned in their other homes became common causes. Sitting at opposite ends of the breakfast table, separated by four noisy children eating homemade yogurt and wheat germ, they felt united by the good deeds they were doing.

Imagery

Some of your images of marriage do not fit the stepfamily, and we have advised you to put these in your attic. Other images, which do fit, can give you energy for your stepfamily. Maybe you have always wanted to be a Boy Scout leader. Now you have three stepsons and a stepdaughter following you around on five-mile hikes. Maybe you and your spouse have had fantasies of opening an inn in the country or adopting six children. Now you feel as if you're hosting an inn with two of your children, two of his, and their assorted friends.

Creating a New Couple Identity

Couples seek validation from the larger community for their marriages. In a second marriage, this approval and support may be hard to find. Your old friends have forsaken you. Your children's friends, parents, and teachers consider you to be Tommy's dad and his new wife. They still remember Tommy's mom. Your coworkers are not comfortable with your new husband.

Finding new friends who know the two of you as *the* couple will help you to feel that your marriage is recognized. You may want to join something together—a racquetball club or a bridge club—just to meet more people with whom you can be social as a couple. Some couples find it useful to form support groups with other remarried pairs. In these groups they are not only accepted as a valid couple; they also receive instant understanding of their dilemmas. One couple took a new last name that had belonged to neither of them and neither of their former spouses. The name symbolized their connection to each other as a new family.

Your extended family can sometimes give support and encouragement to you and your spouse. If they welcome your second partner, you will both feel more comfortable at family occasions and will enjoy sharing your children with their grandparents, aunts, uncles, and cousins. If they are critical of your second marriage, reject your new wife, or continue to talk about your first wife in front of the two of you, you may have to choose between setting them straight about your new family and seeing them less often. A good talk with your family members can educate them about how hard it is for you and your spouse to hear about their contact with your ex-spouse and their worry about the children. They may not realize they are being insensitive. Old friends who still see both you and your former spouse may also need to be informed about your expectations of them.

Intimacy

The Random House College Dictionary lists among its definitions of the word intimacy: "2. a close, familiar, and usually affectionate or loving personal relationship" and "3. a detailed knowledge or deep understanding of a place, subject, period of history, etc."[6] In a marriage, these two meanings of intimacy come together. You and your spouse are close, familiar, and usually affectionate or loving. You also acquire a deep understanding of each other.

One way you acquire deep understanding is by seeing each other as unique individuals. Your wife is not just a pretty brunette. To know each other intimately, you have to strip away your misperceptions and stereotypes. Maybe you grew up in a town where all the men went hunting every fall. You are surprised when hunting season comes around. Your husband possesses neither a hunting license nor a gun. As you take in this new information (you always assumed he would hunt), you gain a greater understanding of his personality, his gentleness, his cowardice, or his willingness to live by his principles even when he is outnumbered.

In a remarriage, you are forced to give up your fantasies and face the reality of the situation. You are not marrying the sweet, virginal girl next door. You may have a struggle to accept the fact that she's already a mother and has had a life with another man. Because you cannot define her by the stereotypes you have used in the past, you must look at her and listen to her more carefully. You have traded romance and fantasy for the opportunity to be intimate.

CHAPTER NINE

The Divorced-Remarried Family

While Marge was living in her single-parent minifamily, before she met Ned, her mother needed major surgery. Marge wanted to spend two weeks with her mother, who lived 1500 miles away, after the operation. She wanted to help her mother get back on her feet. She called her ex-husband, Peter, to see if he could take the children for that time. Peter talked with his second wife, Jessica, and they agreed it would be okay. Jessica had two daughters from her own first marriage. She called her ex-husband to see if he could switch his visitation weekend so it would come after Peter's kids had gone home, rather than in the middle of their stay. He thought to himself, "I am expected to change my plans because my ex-wife's second husband's ex-wife's mother is ill." He did agree to change weekends, however, and called the new woman in his life to rearrange a ski weekend they had planned.

When two parents remain involved with their children, their nuclear family is transformed but not eliminated by their divorce. The adults remain linked to each other through caring for the same children. When they remarry or start living with new adults, those adults also join the team of adults who give care to the children. We call the larger group of people who are caretakers of one set of children the divorced-remarried, or div-rem, family. The div-rem family can consist of two stepfamilies, if both parents are remarried, or one stepfamily and one single parent or visiting minifamily. If the members of a couple each have children from another marriage, they are linked to two div-rem families, his and hers, as well.

The div-rem family is different from a nuclear family. The children, not the adults, are its core. The family is held together by the attachment of the adults to the children. It is also similar to other families in several ways:

Biological ties between parents and children are important.

Financial exchanges take place.

Major transitions affect all the family members.

Members of biological families sometimes joke about seeing each other only at weddings and funerals. In the same way, when there is a crisis or a celebration, you will know that your partner's former spouse is part of your div-rem family.

The members of the div-rem family must face the issues of acceptance, authority, power, and cooperation as the family develops.

ACCEPTANCE

When two parents who are now in two different marriages continue to care for their children, their new stepfamilies become interdependent. Learning to live with and accept this connection is difficult, especially in the beginning. It's hard enough to accept that marrying a divorced person means forming a relationship with his or her children. It's even harder to accept that the marriage also means you will have a relationship with his or her former spouse.

Sometimes the new spouse wants to be accepted and recognized by the former spouse, who is a senior and powerful member of the div-rem family. You don't like feeling that you are invisible when your wife's ex-husband walks by you and fetches his children. When you entertain your stepchildren for the whole summer—and take the trouble to write their mother in Louisiana a letter telling her what they have been doing, the illnesses they have been nursed through, and the clothes you have bought for them—you would like an acknowledgment of your efforts.

Don't be surprised if your letter is not answered. The former spouse, especially if he or she is not in a new marriage or relationship, often finds it hard to accept the new stepparent as a family member. Remember, he or she is not ignoring you as a person; you might be the best of friends if you were on the same bowling team. You are being regarded as "that woman," "his new wife," or "what's her name." You are a symbol of changes over which the former spouse has no control but which nonetheless affect his or her life drastically.

A large part of the relationship between first and second spouses takes place in the imagination. You imagine that the children's mother didn't pack their pajamas because she wanted you to be embarrassed when they had to sleep in their underwear during your mother's visit. When your son criticizes you for drinking too much, you imagine that his stepfather has been telling him you're a bum. When your wife's ex-husband gets his kids for the weekend, you think he comes late on purpose to annoy you.

Unfortunately, your fantasies are not often checked against reality. You have few opportunities to talk directly with your partner's first spouse if you are a stepparent, or with your partner's new spouse if you are the ex-spouse. Direct communication between the former and present spouses can often clear up such difficulties. Some families use counseling to clear the air of misunderstandings. Others (after some time) are able to get together to discuss the children. Sometimes they discover that the children have been creating wrong impressions or omitting information.

The idea of sitting down to talk with your former spouse and his or her new mate may seem absurd to you now. However, most divorced couples who are now able to talk to each other directly and calmly would have had the same reaction several years earlier. You probably once thought the idea that your marriage could end in divorce was also absurd. And you never believed you'd meet someone new and try another marriage.

Feelings of competition are very common between the parent and stepparent of the same sex. You think his new wife is trying to win the children over and turn them against you by sewing and cooking for them. She thinks she is handicapped by coming in late in their lives and being a stepmother. She tries hard because she's number two.

The competition is primarily in your mind. Neither one of you is going to win any prizes. There is no law of nature that says children can love or receive love from only one adult of each sex. They probably benefit from having both of you as helpers and models.

You may feel hurt that although you, the stepmother, care for your stepdaughter on a daily basis, she chooses a nicer gift for her mother than she does for you. You may feel jealous because she calls her mother and chats about the things she's done in school that day while she gives you a cold stare after school. The child may be giving her mother nicer gifts because she feels guilty about living with you. Maybe she is using you to act out her need to become independent. Chatting with her mother is not threatening to her autonomy because she can only reach her mother by telephone. If you take children's actions at face value, you cannot have the objectivity you need to help them grow up. If you want appreciation for what you are doing, you must seek it from the girl's father. Let him buy you the special presents because you are helping him to provide a good home for his child.

Being a stepparent gives you an opportunity to become a more generous person, even against your will. You give to your stepchildren out of responsibility. Because you cannot expect the rewards that a parent gets, you are forced to be altruistic rather than merely giving in order to get some benefit in exchange. Many of us have never had the desire to be as unselfish, patient, and beneficent as we learn to be when we become stepparents.

Sometimes meeting the real "other woman" or "new man" can dispel your jealousy. One divorced mother was very nervous about attending a school conference with her former husband and his second wife, whom she had never met. Afterward she felt relieved:

> You know, I haven't seen Christopher with another woman since the first months of our separation. And then it wasn't Elsa [his second wife]; it was some other woman. But I thought I would feel the same way—nervous and upset. It wasn't like that at all. I'm not upset. And Elsa is not at all like I imagined her. She's just ordinary-looking. I think she's even nice. Not that I would want to be more friendly than this. But I'm glad the whole thing is over, too.

Six-year-old Jonathan wanted to invite his new stepbrother, four-year-old Noah, to his birthday party. Jonathan's mother, Karla, was a little nervous about including her ex-husband's new wife's child, but she agreed to do it because it seemed so important to Jonathan. When Noah arrived, it quickly became clear that he and his mother assumed both of them would stay for the party. Karla was uncomfortable but managed to be a good hostess. The next time she called her ex-husband about arrangements for Jonathan, Noah's mother thanked her again for the party and complimented her on the cake she had baked. Communication between the two women became much easier. Each had put aside her feelings of discomfort in order to please the two children. Now they had a common experience to draw them together.

The relationships between first and second spouses, if they become cordial, do so a little bit at a time. The first time you meet at a school play, you may feel like dropping through the floor. The next time it is a little easier to say hello. By the twentieth time (if your children are young, you may live that long), you are smiling at each other naturally.

AUTHORITY AND POWER

One link between the different parts of the div-rem family is the need to coordinate both your activities with the children and your decisions about their care. A divorce agreement leaves many details to be worked out as you go along. The parent with custody may seem to have more authority than the visiting parent. The visiting parent, however, has power, if his or her cooperation is needed to implement plans, if he or she is providing financial support, or if he or she has a large influence on the children.

There are many situations in which you, the parent, or you, the remarried couple, are not as autonomous as you would like:

- You want to plan a trip for Christmas vacation and take the children along. You have to work this out with their father.

- You think your daughter should get some therapy because she seems to have an eating disorder. You ex-wife has to give her consent.

- You and your husband want to move to the country and build your own house. You can only do this if your former husband will agree to have the children live with him for a year while you are getting settled.

When your former spouse wants to make plans and changes, he or she also has to consult you.

Your former wife calls to say she's having your children (who seem happy to you) evaluated for psychological problems and she wants the bill sent to your insurance plan.

Your ex-husband calls to ask if you will share the cost of sending your son to a private school next year.

Your ex-wife calls to tell you that she's having a baby. She wants to be sure the children can stay with you when she goes to the hospital. Since due dates are always approximate, she expects you to commit yourself to being available for an entire month, on ten minutes' notice

In a stepfamily, these are the realities of your life. Your family is intricately connected to one or two other families. How can you prevent these intrusions, demands, changes, and dependencies from getting in the way of your second marriage?

- Make it a rule to consult your new spouse before you say yes to your former mate. When Anne was evicted from her apartment and called Rick at work to ask him to take the children for a few days, he left straight from his office to get them. Rosayln felt excluded and dumped upon, although they both knew that if Rick had called and asked what she thought, she would have said, "Get the kids." She would have preferred going along for the ride and being a part of the decision making to staying home alone keeping dinner warm.

- Make decisions about the children's care and schedules as a couple.

- Look at all the options you have in a situation as well as the limitations set by the former spouse. If she insists that the children stay with her for Christmas, you can celebrate New Year's with them, leave town for a week, have Christmas a week early in your house, or have a big, grown-up party on Christmas Day. You are not limited to sulking and feeling sorry for yourself and angry at your ex-wife.

- Keep the boundary firm between your stepfamily and your former spouse. This may mean:

  Limiting the time and extent of phone calls.

  Saying no to favors.

  Not asking him or her for favors.

  Putting your schedule down on paper for as many months in advance as possible.

  Working out your own backup arrangements. If you think your former husband will be late getting the children and you and your present husband have an appointment you don't want to miss, hire a baby-sitter to stay with the children until he does arrive for them. You could also leave them at a neighbor's and put a note on your door.

- Ask your ex-spouse to find resources other than you.

- Teach the children what to do in emergencies, how to reach you at work if they need to, what to do if they are locked out of one of their houses, and similar survival skills. Then, if you do not trust your former spouse, you can feel confident knowing that the children can fulfill some of their own needs.

Power Issues

When you are divorced, you have no guidelines for resolving differences between you and your ex-spouse. Some couples do, in fact, write into the agreement the name of a mediator or arbitrator they will consult in case of disputes. Most people hope for the best. The ability of the formerly married couple to cooperate and negotiate, with respect for each other, sets the atmosphere for the div-rem family. If the former spouses are still acting out revenge upon each other from the marriage, it will be hard for a new spouse to feel kindly toward the ex-spouse. If, however, the formerly married couple are able to talk reasonably, compromise, and be flexible with each other, the entire div-rem family will get along more amicably.

A remarried spouse may feel caught between his former wife and his new wife. The man in the middle has loyalties to both women. Their differing needs and priorities can become two sides in an ongoing argument, and he vacillates between them. Sometimes when his former wife gets remarried and no longer needs as much support from him, he can commit himself more easily to an alliance with his second wife.

When both divorced spouses are remarried, the custodial couple usually consider themselves the major parents and take the initiative in planning and decision making. The visiting couple, however, are not always willing to accept a lower status merely because they see the children for less time. They are often the custodial couple for another set of children and are accustomed to being in charge.

The two couples can become competitive or jealous. You may feel you are in a contest to see who are the better parents, the bigger spenders, the more insightful, or the more physically fit. Instead of working together to resolve your differences so the children will have a consistent set of rules and expectations, you are battling for the children's favor and for power within the div-rem family.

The "blood ties" of the biological parents are matched against the effort and investment of the stepparent. The stepfather feels that he should have a greater say in his stepchild's upbringing because, "I do so much for his kid. I spend more time with him than his father does. Why should he decide everything?" The father, feeling deprived because he cannot see the child as much as he would like, says, "I can't see him all the time, but I'm still his father. I have to have some control over how he's brought up."

This kind of conflict has no right answer. Do you support one or the other of these men in your mind? If so, is it because you are in the same position as one of them or married to someone who is? The existence of the div-rem family is a fairly recent phenomenon. Many unresolved moral and ethical questions are raised by the sharing of children between two different homes.

Power conflicts are resolved either by forming a cooperative child care system or by having one couple retain most of the control. Either solution can result in the reduction of open conflicts between former spouses or between stepfamilies. What probably helps the child most is the easing of tension in the adults he or she lives with and visits. When there is less conflict, the adults can focus on the child's needs and on building their family.

COOPERATION

The two sets of parents are able to cooperate with each other when they accept their mutual concern for the children, no longer see each other as primarily interested in taking advantage of them, and give up fighting for the position of most powerful adult or couple.

You may realize from time to time that the div-rem family has some helpful aspects. You are glad your son can be with his father while you and your husband have a vacation alone. You feel you're getting the better end of the deal, and so does he. You find it helpful that your ex-husband's new wife has volunteered to have your daughter's birthday party at her house this year. You see your son's face light up when all four of you come to visiting day at his camp, and you hear him say to his counselor as he looks at all of you, "Awesome."

Cooperation in the div-rem family means flexible reciprocity. You may still trade child-care time and do favors for each other, but you are not as apt to keep track or feel cheated as you were earlier. You don't mind if your husband takes the children for an extra weekend while his dad is visiting because you know the time will come when he'll want to skip a weekend. Your relationship with the children is secure enough to let them spend a little extra time away.

By this time, maybe three to four years following your remarriage, you are responding to your former spouse primarily as "the parent of my children." You and your former spouse may have changed and matured so that you no longer play the same games with each other as you did right after the separation. He sends his check on time. She remembers to pack the children's pajamas. Or your former spouse may still be pushing the same buttons, but you don't react as strongly as you did before. He's still late with the check, but you know it will come eventually so you don't panic. She still forgets to pack the pajamas, but you keep some extras at your apartment. Changes and misunderstandings are not a big deal.

Your stepfamily is likely to be in the affection stage by now. It is easier to be flexible when you and the children are accustomed to each other and know how to get along. You don't regard keeping your stepson an extra weekend as punishment, and you know he won't forget you if he's gone for a month.

When three or four parents have learned how to be cooperative parents, they can work together to help the children. Some div-rem families plan joint celebrations for a graduation or confirmation. They may pool their money for one big gift. One family had a combined Thanksgiving dinner that included the previously married couple, the new live-in partners of each of them, his son from a marriage before that, their two children from their marriage together, and her daughter from her current relationship.

Solving Children's Problems

In one family a girl of nine was not eating. She was using eating habits as a way of manipulating her parents and stepparents. She wanted them to bribe her to eat her food. The mother, stepfather, father, and stepmother had a joint meeting about the problem. They agreed on what they would say to her and how much they would push her to eat. They set up a time to check in with each other to see how their plan was working in each household. The result was a consistent way of handling a difficult problem. In spite of the child's manipulations, each adult felt a responsibility to the others to follow the guidelines they had all set down. The child no longer had anyone willing to engage in a power struggle with her. Her eating problem was soon resolved.

The advantages to working together as a div-rem family are many:

- You have more information about the child's behavior in two homes.
- You have more ideas about how to solve the problem.
- You have the moral support of the other adults. (If you are not remarried, this may be especially helpful.)
- You are not as easily manipulated by the child.

- The child perceives his or her environment as consistent and caring.
- The child cannot benefit or act out by setting you against the other stepfamily.
- If your plan does not work, you know it is not because the other parent and stepparent were not supportive.
- If professional help seems indicated, you are all more likely to agree to it because you have all been aware of the problem.

LACK OF COOPERATION

Don't give up if your div-rem family is not working cooperatively. Your stepfamily life is not doomed to failure because you and your former spouse cannot work out your conflicts. Consider these questions:

1. How long has it been since your divorce? It may be that you are impatient and things will improve.
2. Did one of you leave the marriage for "someone else"? Is that someone else now a second wife or husband? If so, you may never reach the stage of cooperation. You and your spouse must work out strategies to cope with the difficulties of your situation and to help the children as best you can. Some of the suggestions above will be helpful.
3. Is your former spouse still single? Sometimes cooperation between households improves greatly when both partners are in new and satisfying relationships. Many remarried couples have been known to consider a little matchmaking for the not yet remarried ex-spouse.
4. How are your children doing? If tensions and conflicts continue between the two parents, the children may feel torn between the two families, and they may develop problems. You need to keep in touch with their teachers, counselors, and other adults in their lives for information they may not be sharing with you.
5. Are you involving the children in your continuing difficulties of communication with your former spouse? If so, please stop.

They have enough problems just growing up. If you could not improve your spouse's behavior while you were married to him or her, how can the children do it now? They are not to blame for one parent who is not responsible.

6. Is your former spouse so far out of the picture that you hear from him or her once a year or less? If so, you are not likely to change that pattern either. Focus on your stepfamily, which is your children's one and only home.

CHAPTER TEN
The New Baby

You hang up the phone after your weekly conversation with your mother, and you are haunted by her question: "When are you thinking of starting a family of your own?"

She has asked you this question regularly since you got married four years ago, but somehow you cannot dismiss it as lightly as you used to. Something inside of you is asking the same question: "Do we dare?"

Your mother-in-law, on the other hand, has warned you of how upset her grandchildren (your stepchildren) will be if they have to adjust to any more changes. Aren't you lucky, she implies, that you have her wonderful darlings to look after and don't need to go through the messy process of producing any babies yourself?

Your own biological clock is ticking away, reminding you that this is one decision you cannot postpone forever.

Planning to have a baby is a big decision for every couple. Having a child dramatically changes your life as an individual and your life as a couple. In the stepfamily the new baby can affect the lives of all the people in the divorced-remarried family. After all, your new baby will be both your children's and your stepchildren's half sibling. Your former spouse's life will be changed by the newcomer's arrival, as will the life of your partner's former spouse.

THE DECISION

As a remarried couple, you can probably think of many reasons why two people in your situation should or should not have a baby.

Yes, you should have a child together because:

Having a baby is a sign of your commitment and love

You want more children

One of you has never been a biological parent

You miss the stepchildren when they are not with you and you want a child whom you do not share with another household

The female partner in your couple is nearing forty

The birth of your child will make your marriage as legitimate and important as the former marriage(s)

Having a child will give you more power in influencing your partner and his or her former spouse

No, you should not have a child together because:

You both already have children

You cannot afford to raise another child

You do not want to start over at the bottle-and-diaper stage when you have already come so far with your older children

Your children and stepchildren will suffer if they have to adjust to a new sibling

You are older now than you were in your first marriage, and you're looking forward to the time when all the children are out of the house

Having a child will interfere with your career

You do not want to risk the pain of separating from another child if this marriage ends in divorce

You fear that a child will hurt your marriage; perhaps you have already experienced this in your previous marriage

No Baby

In a few cases, the decision is easy. You are too old, or one of you has undergone sterilization. You are a parent, and your partner does not want to be a parent. Even if it is clear that you are not going to have children together, don't be surprised if you have occasional fantasies about having a love child. These daydreams are a sign of the strength of your love. Mourning the loss of that potential child is helpful for your relationship. It may be as simple as a conversation in which you acknowledge, "If we were only younger, we could have had the cutest, brightest, most athletic, most popular children you have ever seen."

Some couples take on projects together in which they share their energy and creativity. They lavish love and attention on the garden, their summer home, the pets, or the slide collection instead of on a child. If you do not have biological children together, you face the challenge of creating a new definition of the family—one that includes children with different ties to each of you.

If you are too old to have children, you can enjoy the pleasures of becoming grandparents together. Your wife's daughter, who was twenty-two when you met, may never call you Dad, but her children won't hesitate to call you Grandpa. As grandparents you can share in caring for children together.

Maybe

If you want children and your partner does not, you may be in for some hard times until you resolve this issue. A second marriage may end in divorce if this difference is not settled. If you are a childless stepparent, you may feel entitled to have a child of your own. If you are an overburdened or burned-out parent, however, you are apt to feel that having another child would be a huge sacrifice.

There is no way to compromise. You can't have half a child; you can't even have a child who will live with you only half the time. You cannot predict, in advance, what having a baby will mean for your stepfamily. You may want to talk with other remarried couples who have and who have not had children. Counseling to resolve this difference is sometimes useful. The rest of this chapter will give you an idea of what may be in store if you choose to have that baby.

Yes

If you both agree readily that you want to have children together, you are ready to move into timing, announcing, and preparing for the new baby.

PLANNING FOR A BABY

Although conception is not an event over which you have complete control, most couples who plan to have children think carefully about when they want the baby to be born.

Timing

In the stepfamily, you are likely to take into account the lives of the stepfamily members in making these plans. Many remarried couples try to minimize the disruption of their lives and their children's lives and maximize the children's contact with the new sibling.

- You may want the baby to be born during the summer, when your older children spend time with you, so they can share the excitement of the baby's arrival.
- You may decide to wait until the children have become accustomed to a new house, the marriage of the other parent, or a major transition before you make another change in their lives.
- You may take into account your financial situation and plan to wait until you can live for some time on only one salary.
- You may want to move into a larger or more convenient home.

Announcing

Some couples share their excitement about the pregnancy with others in their lives as soon as they know. Others wait until they are past the danger of a miscarriage. They then broadcast the news to all their friends and relatives.

In a second marriage you are apt to think carefully about whom to tell, in what order to tell people, and when to tell them. For example:

> If you tell the children first, your former spouse will be upset that you did not tell her first so she could help them adjust to the news.

> If you tell your former spouse first, you may miss the pleasure of telling your children about a major event in your family.

> If you tell your relatives before you tell the children, the children may find out from them.

> If you have children who visit and children who reside with you most of the time, you probably want to tell them all at the same time.

Many parents wonder how far in advance to tell their children about the pregnancy. Giving them as much notice as possible is usually helpful. Young children are likely to forget about the baby when it does not appear in a week or two. You may have to tell them repeatedly until the pregnancy is quite apparent. Knowing about the pregnancy five or six months before the due date is useful for the children. It gives them time to ask questions and get accustomed to the idea. Moreover, if you are keeping a secret from them, they are likely to sense it and have their own theories about what the secret is.

You may be surprised by the children's reactions. Some very basic questions about where the baby is coming from and how it is made are not unusual even from children who, you have assumed, already know the facts of life. This is an opportunity for some good sex education in your home.

Your children may have some unrealistic expectations about the baby. Your four-year-old suggests sharing a bunk bed with the new baby. Your ten-year-old wants to know how soon she can baby-sit. Their negative reactions may include fears that the baby will break their toys, worries that you will neglect or stop loving them, or a sense of shock that you would even think of having a child "at your age."

Preparing

Preparations for a baby can include rearranging your home, your time, and your work life. All these changes will affect the existing children as well.

SPACE

Most parents in nuclear families do not hesitate to have their children share a room. However, many divorced and remarried parents will not consider putting the new baby's crib in the room with their older child. Since the age difference is apt to be five to fifteen years, there are some realistic problems about room sharing.

Providing a room for the new baby may involve moving around one or more of the older children. One eight-year-old was happy to move his things into the room that had been his dad's study and to fix the room so he could use it on his weekend visits. When he realized that his old, small room was being prepared for the baby, however, he became angry and withdrawn.

TIME

During your pregnancy you need to rest, prepare for the needs of the baby, tie up loose ends at work, and learn or review childbirth techniques. You may find it hard to keep up your usual activities with your children. You may ask their other parent to take them more of the time, expect them to care for themselves more, or ask your spouse or extended family to help out. The children may see this as the first step in a path that will take you away from them completely.

WORK

Although the majority of mothers in the United States work outside of their homes, many women either take time off when they give birth to a child or lighten their work schedules. In planning how to adjust your work schedule, you are likely to think about: financial needs, the needs of the baby, the availability of reliable child care, the needs of your older children, and your own desire to be with your children. If your entire time at home is spent caring for the infant, whose cries cannot be ignored, the older children will feel neglected and resentful.

THE COUPLE'S EXPERIENCE

In a stepfamily one or both adults have already had the experience of adding a baby to a previous family. The expectations or associations that each of you has with pregnancy may differ considerably. For example, Albert was unusually shaken about touring the hospital labor room with his pregnant second wife. He was reminded of his older daughter's birth. The baby's life had been in jeopardy. He had felt very frightened and helpless. His wife had felt inadequate when she could not go through with her plans for a natural childbirth. After the delivery, she became depressed and distant from him. Albert sometimes considered this postpartum period the beginning of the end of his first marriage.

Albert could not tell his current wife, Tricia, why he was upset. She thought of nothing but the new baby and always hated to hear about his first marriage. Fortunately, he did talk to his brother about his feelings and realized it was not surprising that the old memories had been aroused. He took some private time to say good-bye again (mentally) to his first marriage. When the time came for Tricia's delivery, he was able to concentrate on her labor and not be haunted by the ghosts of the past.

When Maria became pregnant in her second marriage, her daughter, Lillian, was nine years old. Maria realized that Lillian was worried about losing her place in the family when the new baby came, and she tried to reassure her by spending some extra time as a minifamily of two. This meant she had less time for her husband. He became tense and worried. If his wife already had so little time for him, what was going to happen when the baby came? The two of them did not discuss their differing priorities. Each partner had his or her own view of the events. Maria was focused on the parent-child minifamily she shared with her daughter; her husband was centered in the couple minifamily. Each blamed the other for not being more supportive and understanding.

Confusion can arise when the baby's birth comes at the same time as other family changes. When Albert's son was born, his older daughter was entering a private high school. Although he had set aside money for her tuition and could handle the increased expenses, he became unusually worried about money during Tricia's pregnancy. He did not know that this reaction is typical of pregnant women's husbands, and he convinced himself that he urgently needed to work longer hours and take on more cases in his law practice. Tricia, isolated at home with the baby, felt resentful that her husband was working more than ever. She assumed he had to work those extra hours to pay his daughter's tuition. She could not imagine that the new baby—who drank breast milk, slept in a borrowed crib, and had his medical expenses covered by insurance—could be the reason her husband was putting in longer hours at the office. She thought Albert felt pressured to pay his daughter's school expenses and she became less willing to have her stepdaughter visit. Albert assumed that Tricia had ceased to like his child now that she had a baby of her own. He became overprotective of the older child as he saw her being pushed out of the family. Tricia, in turn, felt Albert was demonstrating that his second family would always come second.

Albert and Tricia illustrate what can happen in any marriage when each member of the couple assumes that he or she knows the reasons for the other person's behavior. Each assumption that is not checked out with the other partner adds to the misunderstanding between them. Often a series of talks in which both partners listen carefully, share their viewpoints, and ask directly about the assumptions they are making can put the relationship back on solid ground.

ADDING A FAMILY MEMBER
The First-Time Parent

Becoming a parent for the first time is a major life change. Most parents cannot even remember what it was like before they had children. In the stepfamily becoming a parent may also have special meanings:

> There was nothing that was mine. When I married Paul, I moved into his house. At least one of his kids has lived with us the whole time we've been together. It's his neighborhood, his friends. But the baby is mine, too. That makes a big difference. [Linda, the stepmother of three teenagers and the mother of an infant.]

> I hate to say this, but having the baby has meant that I don't try so hard to please my stepson, Peter. I know there's a little one who'll smile at me and let me give him all the hugs I want to. I don't feel that I need Peter's affection as much. Funny thing is he's taking more initiative with me. He sees me playing with the baby, and the next thing I know he's leaning against me or trying to climb into my lap. [Ivan, the stepfather of an eight-year-old and the father of a one-year-old.]

Disappointments

The birth of a child may bring all the images of what a family should be tumbling down from the attic where we stored them in Chapter Five. You want your first child to be the center of attention. You want your husband to camp out in the hospital with you, like the other new fathers in the childbirth class. You don't want your stepchildren (who suddenly look like giants by comparison) touching the baby with their dirty hands. You want the grandparents to be fussing and bragging about your baby. You may feel angry or hurt that the spotlight continues to be shared with the children from the previous marriage.

As a first-time father you feel less adequate and confident than your partner, who already has children. You are all thumbs as you hold this squirmy little bundle, afraid that any minute it will start to scream. When your wife (who has already mothered three children) holds him, she looks relaxed and casual. You keep checking the baby every five minutes. Is he wet? Is he cold? Is he hot? Is he happy? Your wife tells you not to worry, babies are sturdy, but you worry anyway. If he were her first child, she might be sharing those concerns with you instead of making you feel like an old worrywart.

Remarried parents and stepparents often become very concerned about "how the children are taking it." Visitors are reminded to bring a "big-brother gift," and the baby is kept almost out of sight while the older child is praised. The younger child may not even have a room of its own for years. Some younger children shift spaces according to the schedule of stepchildren. First-time parents can find themselves feeling resentful that, even with *their* first child, they have to cope with sibling rivalry.

Lopsided Attachments

Stepfamily issues of acceptance, authority, and affection do not disappear with the coming of a new baby. Anxiety about acceptance may reemerge because there is now a new category of membership. Having another child may upset the balance of attachments among the family members.

As a remarried parent, you are suddenly struck by a ton of guilt when you realize how disrupted your older children's lives have become. They've been late for school twice this week because you forgot to prepare their lunches. They can't sleep late on the weekends because the baby is up at 5 a.m. You can't help them with their homework without interruptions from the infant. You try to make it up to them by giving their more attention. Your husband responds by taking over the baby when he's home and paying less attention to his stepchildren. Your family is again splitting into minifamilies.

A stepmother who was previously childless and chooses to nurse her baby may unconsciously exclude her husband from caring for the new child just as she has felt excluded from his special relationship with his children.

The older children contribute to the imbalance by making more demands on the parent to do things without the new baby. They want to go to baseball games, appear in school plays, or play catch in the park. You soon learn that you cannot shoot baskets with the baby in a pack on your back or keep the infant from crying in a movie theater. A remarried couple may have been able to attend a child's school play together before the baby came. Now the stepparent will probably stay home so they can avoid the cost of a sitter for the new baby.

The Second-Time-Around Parent

You are excited about the new baby. Your children are even excited and happy that you are pregnant. The baby arrives. Your life is a whirlwind of confusion. Sometimes you look at your older children—the ones who have struggled with you through the divorce, the days of being a single parent, the initial stages of the stepfamily—and you feel sad. If only they could have had the security this little one has. If only you could have given them what you can give now. You never thought having a baby would bring up all this sorrow and guilt again.

Most parents have these pangs. They do pass. Comparisons between the past and the present are inevitable. Nonetheless, you cannot avoid feeling pulled between the two children or two sets of children. They need you differently because of the differences in their ages and the different histories they have had with you. Trying to be "fair" is meaningless. Trying to be responsive to them without neglecting yourself is more realistic.

You cannot make up for the past by overcompensating now. Don't try so hard to keep your life with your older children unchanged that you find yourself exhausted and short-tempered with everyone. Remember, being the parent of an infant or toddler is harder at thirty-five than at twenty-five.

It is easy to become so caught up in the needs of your various children and stepchildren that you forget to take care of yourself. If you feel neglected, have not had a quiet conversation with another adult or any time alone in days, you are not likely to be a patient, flexible, nurturant parent or spouse. If you can't remember the last time you treated yourself to a meal out, a haircut, or a walk around the block without the children, it's time to do something for yourself.

Relationships Among the Children

Children who have one parent in common are half siblings. Your children from your first marriage and your spouse's children from the prior marriage are stepsiblings to each other. They are all half brothers or half sisters of the child you have in your second marriage.

Having a child in your second marriage sometimes seems to bring the whole family together. The couple's home is now permanently the home of at least one child. Two sets of stepsiblings are both related to the new baby. They seem to be brought closer by knowing this. It is also likely that by the time the remarried couple are ready to have a child together, they have reached the affection stage of their stepfamily and the family members are already feeling more united.

Your older children are apt to have ambivalent reactions to the new brother or sister. They may be excited, they may like the new child and enjoy being looked up to by the little brother or sister. They may also feel jealous and displaced. The fact that a child is already eight, nine, ten, or sixteen does not eliminate the possibility that feelings of jealousy may arise. Don't be surprised by statements such as these:

"Who said the baby could use *my* high chair?" [A ten-year-old who has been too big for the high chair for the last seven years.]

"Those are my dolls she's playing with." [A twelve-year-old who threw those dolls on the closet floor and didn't notice when you moved them to the attic.]

"You love the baby more than me because you divorced my daddy and you still love his daddy."

"It's not fair that she [the baby] lives here seven days a week and I'm only here two days."

"It's no fun going shopping with you anymore, Mom. All we do is chase Jimmy [toddler half brother] so he won't get lost."

Although the children's fears and jealousies are not always logical, they reflect a genuine fear of being replaced in your heart. They fear that you will prefer the child of your current spouse just as you love your new partner more than the one you divorced. When both of an older child's biological parents are remarried and have new families, the child may feel like an outsider in both homes.

The same older children may also be very generous. Your stepson comes for a visit laden down with outgrown toys for his baby brother. Your teenage daughter volunteers to baby-sit every weekend. The children appreciate the baby's interest in them, how she follows them around, smiles at them, or learns to mispronounce their names. As the half brother or half sister grows up a little, the older sibling can show him or her off to friends. They can do favors for each other; they can enjoy playing hide-and-seek or digging in the sand together.

For some children whose parents were unhappily married or divorced when they were quite young, having a half sibling provides a chance to relive some of their past in happier circumstances. They enjoy watching a younger child get the love and attention they missed out on. Somehow the caring rubs off on them. They learn that a child does not mean the end of a marriage.

Painful memories can also arise:

"Why didn't Grandma come to my birthday party when I was three? She's coming to Terry's?"

"How come you made me go to day care till five o'clock and Terry only goes in the morning?"

"Terry sure is lucky you guys aren't always fighting the way you and my dad used to when I was little."

"By the way, Mom, exactly how old was I when you and Dad got divorced?"

Although, as a parent, you would rather not hear about the past, you can help your child by talking openly about his or her earlier years and about your divorce. In this way, you help children to become freer psychologically from the effects of those earlier experiences.

Problem Solving

If problems arise with your marriage or your older children following the birth of a new child, here are some steps to take in tracing the source of the difficulty.

1. Define the problem very carefully. The whiny, sullen behavior that you label jealousy may reflect problems at school, an illness, or your child's age.
2. Check with your child's other parent, teachers, or child-care providers to see if they observe the same problem behavior as you.
3. Talk about the problem with the family member involved. Does your wife mean to keep you away from the baby, or is she trying to make sure you don't feel burdened by caring for another child on your time off?
4. Think about changes that have taken place in your family. Have you changed your child-care schedule or routines? Is the child picked up at school by car pool these days, instead of by you?
5. How are you handling the changes in your family? Are you tired, grumpy, worried about money, inattentive some of the time? Could this be affecting the other members of your family?

When you have clarified the specific problem, you may discover that the new sibling is not causing the difficulty. In any case, using your problem-solving skills and strategies will help you feel more competent as a family leader.

RESPONSES OF THE DIV-REM FAMILY

Even if you have been divorced and remarried for years, you may feel strange when you learn that your former wife or your former husband's second wife is expecting a baby. Memories and ties from the past may still tug at you unexpectedly.

As a parent you may be concerned about the effects of your ex-spouse's new baby on your children. Will they receive the care they need once the new baby comes? Will the new child be used as an excuse for your ex-spouse to see the children less frequently or contribute less financial support? Some of the fears parents have are realistic and others are exaggerated.

If your former spouse has a good relationship with the children, he or she will probably continue to care for them in the same manner. If the connection between a visiting parent and children has been weak, the new baby's arrival can mark either a further deterioration or an improvement in their relationship. Instead of making gloomy predictions, it is important to assess the changes as they occur and help your child adjust.

When div-rem family members are able to cooperate, they are less likely to feel threatened by new siblings. Some former spouses bring gifts to the new child and help in its care. One father of fourteen-year-old twins from his first marriage asked his former wife if the twins could watch his four-year-old at her house for a weekend while he and his second wife attended a conference. His former wife agreed, and she enjoyed the weekend as much as the three children did.

UNEXPECTED QUESTIONS

Children born to remarried parents have unique views of family life. Most parents do not anticipate the questions they find themselves answering:

"When I'm bigger, will I go somewhere else on the weekends?"

"Why can't I have a mommy and a stepmommy like Betsy?"

"Don't you think it would be fun if I had six grandparents, too?"

"How can Tommy be part of our family today but not yesterday?"

"Why doesn't Betsy bring her real mommy with her when she visits us?"

Ten-year-old Jack spent weekdays with his mother and week-ends with his father. His father had remarried when Jack was three, and now he had two younger children, Teddy, who was four, and Sharon, who was one. When Sharon was born, Teddy had begun to sleep in Jack's bedroom on the nights when Jack was not there so the baby's crying would not wake him. On the weekends Teddy moved back into his own bed in the room he shared with Sharon. Although Teddy spent more time in Jack's room than Jack did, it remained "Jack's room" in decor and in the family's vocabulary.

Teddy's mother, Jane, noticed that Teddy became disruptive and aggressive on the weekends when Jack visited and tried to compete with his little sister for attention. One day she heard a spot on the radio about "middle children." She realized that Teddy was an oldest child during the week and a "middle child" on weekends. He could not compete with Jack's competence or break into the special relationship Jack had with his father, so he tried to displace the baby instead.

When Sharon was a year old, she would point at Teddy when her mother asked, "Where's brother?" If Jane pointed at Jack, Sharon laughed.

Teddy heard Jack calling his father Dad and his mother Jane. He tried calling his mother Jane and was told to call her Mommy. The next time Jack came for a visit and called his stepmother Jane, Teddy said, "No, you're wrong. Her name is Mommy."

Jane and her husband, Larry, had started explaining the family relationships to the children when Teddy was still a baby, but it took several years for the connections to be clear to the younger children. They asked the same questions repeatedly until they were ready intellectually to comprehend the answers.

It is best not to hide any information from your children. A child in Teddy's position can be told that he and Jack have the same dad and different mothers. He can accept this information because he does not have an image of family firmly rooted in his mind. It helps for the children of the second marriage to meet the other parent of their half siblings if it is at all possible. They sometimes meet at a transition time, a soccer game, or a graduation party. The younger child also likes to see the older child's other house and other room. Then, when the older child is not in the stepfamily home, the half sibling has a mental image of the other's environment

Half siblings can become very attached to each other. The younger children often miss the older child when he or she is in another home or at school. They enjoy the attention the older child gives them and the excitement that often accompanies his or her visit. The half sibling sometimes introduces the younger child to new experiences or new ideas. Having such a big brother or sister is also a source of pride. When Teddy overheard some boys in his nursery school bragging about their older brothers, who were six and seven, he announced, "My big brother is ten."

CHAPTER ELEVEN
Six Stepfamilies and Their Stories

*I*f you have been remarried for a number of years, think back to the beginning of your stepfamily. Have there been any changes since then in the children's visiting schedule or the financial arrangements for child support? Do you feel differently about your stepfamily now or think of it in a new way? Have you changed your opinion of your stepchildren or your partner's former spouse? Do you now act differently with the members of your stepfamily?

If you answered yes to one or more of these questions, your family is not unusual. All families change and develop over time. Stepfamilies seem to change even more because they have more members and those members must make a series of transitions to form the stepfamily. These transitions do not ordinarily occur quickly or smoothly. Often a change in one minifamily results in a change in another minifamily. Waves of change move back and forth between households, affecting a series or relationships.

In this chapter you will read about the changes that took place in several stepfamilies. In some of the families, change took place with relative ease. In others, a child experienced some hard times during the change process. In these family descriptions the focus is on (1) the minifamilies and (2) the role of a stepparent or New Person in bringing about change, either knowingly or by chance.

Your family will not be exactly like any of the ones described, but you may find yourself and your children or spouse reflected in parts of their stories. When you have finished, you may want to think about the history of change in your family. Seeing how far you have come may make you feel hopeful about the future.

CHANGING OLD PATTERNS

Pete and Gloria were divorced after twelve years of marriage when their sons, Glen and Stan, were ten and seven years old, respectively. Gloria had custody of the children. Pete was to pay a fixed amount of child support each month and to have liberal visiting arrangements with the boys. Gloria and Pete agreed that the terms of their divorce were fair and reasonable.

The Divorce Agreement

The former-spouse minifamily had some problems in keeping this agreement. Pete became habitually late in sending the child support payments to Gloria. She expressed her frustration by preventing Pete from seeing the children. This was actually a variation on an old pattern between them. During their marriage Pete had often withheld care, money, or protection and Gloria had responded by withholding affection, nurturance, or sex. After the divorce, money was the only commodity Pete could still withhold.

Although Gloria was no longer expected to be affectionate or nurturant toward her ex-husband, she used the children as an extension of herself in preventing his contact with them. Pete's fear of being cut off from his sons would finally motivate him to pay the child support. His withholding was (unconsciously) a way of testing whether his ex-wife still "cared" about his provisions for the family. He found that she did care because he could provoke her anger by his behavior.

A New-Couple Minifamily

Several years after the divorce, Gloria's new friend, David, moved in with her and the boys. David's entrance into the div-rem family affected Gloria's behavior in her minifamily with Pete. She was now in a relationship that was not based on each person's withholding from the other. When David moved in, he agreed to share the household expenses. Gloria became less dependent on the child support money from Pete. She was less disturbed when Pete failed to send the money on time, and she did not block his visits with the boys. In fact, the children's visits with their father took on a new meaning for Gloria: They provided time for her to be alone with David.

Pete's Response

Several months after David moved in, Pete was two weeks late in sending the child support payment. He was relieved that Gloria didn't nag him about it. The next month, when he was ten days overdue in sending the check, he started getting depressed. He found himself waiting for the phone to ring, anticipating Gloria's angry call, his defensive arguments, a special trip to her house to deliver the check, and a familiar feeling of intensity and excitement.

When Gloria did not call, he felt lost and lonely. He considered not seeing his children at all, now that their mother had ceased trying to stop him from seeing them. He thought of asking for more visitation time to make up for his loneliness and, perhaps, to start another argument. Finally, he took out his checkbook, looked at the balance, wrote Gloria's check, and mailed it at the corner. He felt dejected and alone, more alone than he had since the initial separation. For the next few weeks he felt himself just drifting along, seeing the children at his appointed times, working during the week, and feeling sorry for himself on weekends.

The Visiting Minifamily

Glen and Stan had to go through the acceptance stage with David slowly. They had grown accustomed to living alone with their mother.

When the boys saw Pete, they knew he was sad. They could identify with him because they, too, were feeling a sense of loss. They discovered ways to cheer up their father. They taught him to play Dungeons and Dragons; they called him between visits to discuss new moves. Pete found a video arcade near his office and took the children there on some of their visits. He and the children began to spend more time together.

Response of the New Couple

David had been a stepchild himself. His divorced mother had remarried when he was thirteen. He had always wished that he could have been closer to his stepfather, who seemed remote and unaffectionate, or his father, who had moved halfway across the country and rarely kept in touch. David had a desire to be a better stepfather to Gloria's children than his stepfather had been to him. He felt rejected when the boys wanted to be out of the house more now that he was there.

Gloria sensed that the children needed to work out their relationship with their father before they could accept a stepfather. She urged David to let the boys do things in their own way. David wanted to prove his ability to be a good stepfather, but he knew that if his father had been as available to him as Pete was to Glen and Stan, he would have wanted to be with him every minute possible. He was able to give the children's needs priority over his own.

While the boys were improving their relationship with their father, Gloria and David took the time to get to know each other better and to relax together.

Changes in the Visiting Minifamily

About a year later, Pete met a new woman, Cynthia. He started spending time with her, both with his children and without them. Glen got an after-school job to earn money so he could buy himself a new bicycle. The boys visited Pete less often, but the strong sense of attachment and commitment among them remained.

Authority Struggles

The boys were able to accept David as a stepfather now that they had demonstrated loyalty to their biological father. In the first few months David had mostly let Gloria discipline the children. When he did say something, they usually listened. As the boys became more used to him and he started to take a greater role in setting limits, each boy went through a period of rebelliousness, testing, and disobedience. "You're not my father. Why should I listen to you?" was heard more than once.

The children's reaction reminded David of his own unspoken anger toward his stepfather. He often gave in to the children because he didn't want them to dislike him. David needed special coaching from Gloria and from his older brother, who had children of his own, to learn to be firm about the limits he set.

Father's Reaction

Pete heard about these hassles when the boys visited him, but he did not get involved. He felt he should let his sons work out their own difficulties with their stepfather.

Pete's relationship with Gloria had calmed down. It was now easy and cordial. When they had differences between them or conflicts about scheduling, they managed to compromise. The support checks were mailed on time, and Pete could see that the boys were well taken care of.

Pete's New Relationship

Pete's new woman friend, Cynthia, had a four-year-old daughter, Abigail, who lived with her. Cynthia did not object to the time that Glen and Stan spent with Pete and sometimes arranged to take one boy somewhere with her while the other one did something special with his dad. In this way she provided each boy with a chance for some one-to-one time with their father.

Glen and Stan tested Cynthia's authority less than they had David's. It was easier for them to accept a second new relationship, and they considered Cynthia and Abigail an added attraction on their visits. They already felt secure in their visiting minifamily with their father. Moreover, now that they were older, their energies were being redirected away from home.

Mother's Remarriage

When Gloria and David announced plans to get married, four years after the divorce, Glen and Stan were initially unhappy. They got along well with David and they could not explain their objections to the marriage plans. Gloria phoned Pete to warn him of the children's moodiness; she explained that they were having difficulties about the marriage. Pete and Cynthia talked to the boys; they discussed how kids feel about a parent's remarriage. They listened to the boys without pushing them to talk.

Cynthia suggested that they plan a special dinner party to celebrate the wedding announcement. Glen, Stan, Pete, Cynthia, and Abigail cooked a special meal for Gloria and David. The four adults and three children had a festive party. This celebration helped the boys to accept the remarriage. By the day of the wedding, they were quite excited about attending. After the wedding Glen told Pete, "I hope you get remarried too. Weddings are fun."

Observations

Here are some of the ways in which this family made changes easier:

David did not interfere when Pete's support checks were late, and Gloria was able to change her reactions to the late payments.

The children were allowed to work out their relationships in each of the new minifamilies separately and on their own terms.

Cynthia respected the boys' need for alone time with their father.

Pete and Cynthia understood the boy's feelings about their mother's remarriage. They offered support both for the children and the other couple.

COMPETITION BETWEEN FATHER AND STEPFATHER

Janet was unhappy with Jerry for many years before she had the courage to ask him for a divorce. Jerry was reluctant to take her seriously. When she asked him to leave the house, he took four months finding an apartment for himself. His slowness bothered her, but she did not know how to be more firm with him.

A Difficult Separation

After Jerry moved out, he came to the house frequently to see his son, Teddy, who was nine, and to be around Janet. During his visits, he preferred to stay in the house, do his laundry, use his old basement workshop, and watch TV with Teddy. He rarely let her know in advance when he was coming or how long he would stay. Janet alternated between angrily asking him to leave her alone and compliantly arranging her life around his. She waited with Teddy for Jerry to come and then left them alone for a while. She never felt that Jerry was dependable enough to stay with Teddy for the entire weekend. She never took off on her own.

The separation resembled the marriage. Jerry liked to be around his wife and son but did not seek intense contact with either of them. Janet, not satisfied with the relationship that Jerry could offer, was ineffective in enforcing the distance she had demanded.

A New Relationship for Janet

Janet taught computer courses for business executives. In one of her classes she met Anthony, a divorced father. Anthony and Janet began to spend a lot of time together.

One Sunday afternoon, when Anthony and his six-year-old son were visiting Janet and Teddy, Jerry showed up with his laundry bag. Janet was about to let him in when Anthony intervened.

"I know this is not my business, but I think you should call your ex-wife first. Now don't disturb us," he told Jerry in a brusque voice.

Jerry was angry but too embarrassed to stay around. From that time on he called before he came. He also gave in to Janet's request for a regular visitation schedule because he wanted to avoid further confrontations with Anthony.

In this way, Anthony helped Janet to set a tighter boundary around her parent-child minifamily with Teddy. This was helpful because it allowed Janet and Jerry to work out a visitation schedule. Janet had been considering moving to another state primarily because she did not know how to limit Jerry's intrusions into her home. On the other hand, Anthony's action meant that Janet and Jerry did not confront each other directly. They never worked out any ground rules for their relationship as coparents.

The Visiting Minifamily

Teddy liked visiting his dad regularly. When they were together in Janet's home, Jerry faded in and out of contact with Teddy. Teddy never knew how long his dad would be there. On their scheduled visits Jerry had to pay more attention to his son, and the times together became more predictable. When Jerry took Teddy to the Little League tryouts, he volunteered to help coach Teddy's team. This created a strong bond between them. They practiced batting and throwing, watched baseball together on TV, and went to local Big League games. Jerry began to enjoy his son and to feel relieved at not spending so much time in Janet's house, as he now defined his former home.

The father-child minifamily, in its own setting, developed into a new and stronger unit. Their shared interest in baseball became a way to expand the relationship. Jerry was better able to be a good father to an active child striving for mastery than to the depressed and frightened Teddy he had seen on his visits in Janet's house. Teddy and Jerry were both excited by their new minifamily.

Son and Stepfather

Rather than work through any of her feelings about Jerry, Janet had pushed him away and relied on Anthony. She had no desire to support Jerry's fathering role. She preferred to have her son transfer his loyalty from his father to his stepfather, as she had done. She preferred not to be reminded of Jerry's presence in her life.

Two years later, Anthony, now married to Janet, started to teach his son, Tony, Jr., to play baseball. He wanted Teddy to join them in practicing. Teddy was initially reluctant to practice with his stepfather and stepbrother, but his interest in baseball and his mother's urging were stronger than his loyalty to his father. He joined in. Janet was pleased to see her new husband and her son getting along; she suggested that Anthony volunteer to coach Teddy's team. He did and arranged for Tony to join the team also.

Jerry was no longer an official coach of the team, but he frequently helped out at games and practice. When he discovered that Anthony had moved in on his territory, he became very angry. However, he could not share this anger with Janet any more easily than he could communicate with her when they were married. Jerry appealed to Teddy to intervene and ask Anthony to quit the coaching position. Teddy became angry and upset. He felt torn between his loyalty to his father and to his mother, who wanted him to accept his stepfather. Like his parents, he was not able to initiate a direct confrontation.

Father's Withdrawal

Without any way in the div-rem family to express his anger or receive help in maintaining the relationship with his son, Jerry felt abandoned by Teddy and Janet. He attended Teddy's ball games less frequently and cut back on his visitation times.

Jerry had recently met a divorced woman who had a child. He began to spend time with them on weekends. Janet felt that Jerry's withdrawal justified Anthony's participation in Teddy's Little League practice.

"If it weren't for you," she said to Anthony, "Teddy would have no one to support him in sports. I'm no athlete."

Child's Reaction

Teddy was hurt and bewildered. He did not understand what had brought about the change in his relationship with his father. He sometimes blamed himself but felt too powerless to make any changes. He missed the time with his father and felt jealous of both Jerry's woman friend's daughter and Anthony's son. Janet and Anthony did not understand the cause of Teddy's depression. They attributed it to his turning eleven. They thought he would outgrow it.

Distance Between Teddy's Two Families

Teddy and Jerry never regained their close relationship. Jerry continued to date his new woman. He finally married her and acted as a father to her child. (Her ex-husband had stopped communicating with her completely.) Teddy sometimes thought about getting to know his dad better but knew that his mother and stepfather would be unhappy if he did. Anthony tried very hard to become a father to Teddy, but there was always a barrier between them. Teddy often felt he did not have a real home. The stepsiblings in both his parents' homes seemed to belong more than he did. When Teddy's depression did not disappear as he entered adolescence, Janet thought he had inherited a lethargic and pessimistic attitude from his father.

Observations

The former-spouse minifamily in this divorced-remarried family never completed the process of moving apart and learning to be coparents. Janet was happy to have Anthony step in between her and her former husband in order to create distance between them. Janet's desire to push Jerry away, without recognizing his role in Teddy's life, undermined the visiting minifamily. Had Jerry been more forceful in personal relationships, he might have been able to form a stronger relationship with his son. His own reticence, however, coupled with Janet's lack of support and Anthony's direct rivalry, resulted in a distant parent-child relationship.

COMPETING NEEDS

Leah and Dwayne divorced after four years of marriage when Jill was two years old. Jill lived with her mother and saw her father frequently.

Mother's Remarriage and Desire for a New Child

When Jill was eleven, Leah married Bruce, a man her age who had never been married. The mother-daughter minifamily had very strong ties, and Bruce found himself feeling isolated and unappreciated for much of their first year together. Jill would demand her mother's undivided attention and complain that things were not the way they used to be with just the two of them. Leah was often unaware that she was not sharing her daughter. The acceptance stage was long and slow.

Bruce and Leah were eager to have a child together. Leah, already in her thirties, felt that time was running out. Bruce wanted the experience of raising his own child. They kept postponing a decision about pregnancy because Jill was having such a hard time. Her mother felt that asking her to adjust to another newcomer so soon would be unfair.

Caring for an Elderly Parent

On Bruce and Leah's first anniversary, they received a call saying that Bruce's father had had a stroke. They visited him regularly in the hospital and, when he was ready to leave, they took him to their home for his convalescence. Bruce, an only child, felt a strong responsibility to his father. Leah wanted to be helpful and thought it reasonable that she put up with Bruce's father, since he had to put up with her daughter. The older man needed a great deal of care and attention.

Jill was very jealous. She felt abandoned by her mother with these two new men in her home.

After nearly a year in their home, Bruce's father had another stroke and died three days later. The stepfamily of Bruce, Leah, and Jill came together at the time of the funeral. Jill was clearly frightened by her first experience with death, and both adults comforted her. She tried to be nicer to Bruce because she felt sympathy for him.

The pregnancy had been postponed during this time. After her father-in-law's death, Leah thought that they all needed time to grieve and get used to their three-person household before they could easily accept another change. She also wanted to spend time with Jill to make up for having been so preoccupied with caring for Bruce's father.

The Visiting Minifamily

During this time Jill had continued to visit her father regularly. She wanted from him the special attention she was unable to get from her mother. Dwayne was living with a new woman, Elissa, whom he was planning to marry. Elissa was thirteen years younger than Dwayne. Jill did not accept Elissa any more easily that she had accepted Bruce. When her father picked her up for visits, she complained about having to sit in the back seat of the car while Elissa sat in the front. She hated Elissa's cooking.

Jill had controlled her expression of anger first at her mother's remarriage and than at her mother's agreeing to care for a sick old man. Her angry feelings about being displaced often came out, however, in moody and demanding behavior with her father.

The New Couple

Jill's behavior was a source of friction between her father and Elissa. Dwayne tended to be indulgent with Jill, since he only saw her on visits. He understood that she was jealous about her mother's remarriage. He thought that if he and Elissa could be especially nice to Jill, she would be more accepting of their own marriage plans when they decided to share them with her.

Elissa considered Jill's behavior rude and babyish. She resented

Jill's close relationship with Dwayne and often felt jealous of the attention he showed her. She did not look forward to spending the rest of her life playing second fiddle to Dwayne's daughter. Elissa also resented the fact that her life was affected by Jill's mother's choosing to care for her father-in-law.

Father's Remarriage Plans

Elissa pushed hard for Dwayne to set a wedding date. Her parents were coming for a visit during the summer. She knew they would not stay with her if she was living with a man to whom she was not married. She also wanted children of her own. The sooner they married, she felt, the sooner they could think about children. She and Dwayne finally set a date and started making plans.

Jill's Preparation for Her Father's Wedding

Jill was very ambivalent when she was told about the wedding. She did not like to think that Elissa, of whom she was jealous, could really become her stepmother. However, she liked the idea of a real wedding (her mother and Bruce had gone to City Hall). She could identify with Elissa, who was only ten years older than she, and imagine the kind of wedding she would want if she were getting married. She enjoyed talking to Elissa about the flowers, color schemes for the dresses, and music for the wedding.

Jill and Elissa spent a day together without Dwayne, buying new clothes for Jill to wear to the wedding. Elissa helped her choose a dress and shoes that were more grown-up and sophisticated than her mother would have allowed. They ate lunch together in a fancy restaurant. Jill was beginning to see some advantages to having Elissa in her family. Dwayne was delighted.

Mother's Reaction

When Leah saw Jill modeling the outfit for her father's wedding, she became furious. She was already overworked and tired from caring for her father-in-law, supporting Bruce, and coping with a recent death. She thought Dwayne was very inconsiderate to plan a wedding at this time. All she had ever heard from Jill about Elissa were complaints. She thought it would be too much of a strain for Jill to accept another stepparent so soon. She also thought that the clothes Elissa has bought Jill were completely inappropriate for a thirteen-year-old, and far too expensive.

All Leah's frustration at having to delay moving ahead in her own family, at not being able to have another baby yet, was directed at Dwayne. Leah feared that if the marriage upset Jill more, she would have to wait even longer. Perhaps she and Bruce would never get to have a family together. Jill would grow up and leave, and she and Bruce would be all alone. It reminded her of the way Dwayne had treated her when they were married. He had spontaneously invited guests for dinner without asking her. Once he had bought a suit with the money she was saving for a washing machine. Incidents she thought she had forgotten started racing through her mind.

Leah's reaction was not unusual. She experienced feelings toward her ex-husband that had not been resolved when they divorced. Again she felt that he had taken the first move while she was forced to take care of Jill. Her anger prevented her from giving Jill any support for coping with the change in her father's life.

Jill's Divided Loyalty

Jill understood her mother's anger and felt more ambivalent herself. If she pleased her father by supporting the wedding, she hurt her mother. If she supported her mother by being angry about the wedding, she disappointed her father and missed out on an exciting event and her new friendship with Elissa. She coped with her dilemma by behaving very differently in each household. At her mother's home she complained about the wedding and having to meet Elissa's family. With her father and Elissa she became more excited and enthusiastic.

The Wedding

The wedding date was six weeks after the death of Bruce's father. Leah was shocked that Jill was looking forward to going. Bruce felt that Jill deserved a change after the hard times they had all been through. He appreciated the way Jill was trying to comfort him.

Jill was a little nervous at the ceremony. She felt a sense of loss as her father kissed Elissa at the end. At the party, however, a cousin of Elissa's who was Jill's age took an interest in her and she was quite flattered. She returned to her mother's house in a bubbly mood, wanting to share what had happened. Leah was so hurt by her daughter's disloyalty that she hardly listened.

An event such as a wedding, which marks a transition in people's lives, can also become a focus for feelings between different parts of the div-rem family. Leah was angry and felt sorry for herself. Her ex-husband was celebrating and she was mourning. Jill's increasing acceptance of Elissa and continuing loyalty to her father were made crystal clear to her mother.

Greater Distance Between Mother and Daughter

That summer Jill chose to spend much more time than usual at her father's home. Her father, Elissa, and the new grandparents could give her more than her burned-out mother and stepfather. Elissa did not object to the frequent visits because suddenly Jill had turned from a sullen, demanding child into a young woman who openly admired Elissa and tried hard to act grown-up. Elissa continued to treat Jill more like a kid sister than a stepchild, and this was a rewarding connection for both of them.

Leah was jealous because Jill was choosing to spend more time with her father. She had planned to spend extra time with Jill herself. Bruce felt relieved that he and Leah had some time alone together. They had a lot of catching up to do.

Bruce convinced Leah to go ahead and become pregnant. By the time the baby was born, they would all feel better. He helped his wife to see that Jill no longer needed to be protected from family changes. In agreeing to Bruce's suggestion, Leah did not even consider what might be happening in Dwayne's new family. She expressed her deepened loyalty to Bruce and to their needs as a couple.

Leah and Jill became less close as result of this series of changes. Although they both felt uncomfortable for several months, it was an appropriate change for a mother and teenaged daughter.

Jill became more secure with both stepfamilies and developed a life focused around her own interests and friends. Changes at home affected her less. When both her parents eventually had new babies, she was hardly jealous.

Observations

Jill's sudden and strong affection for Elissa was unusual. Stepmothers who are considerably younger than the children's father are often rejected. Elissa's best decision was not to be motherly but to act as a big sister. Jill was so much in need of encouragement to grow up that Elissa's help was greatly appreciated. By treating Elissa like an older sister, Jill felt that she was able to preserve her close relationship with her mother.

Leah had continued to postpone her own gratification by concentrating on the needs of the other people in her family. Bruce helped her change this pattern by creating a new couple relationship in which their needs were shared rather than competitive. He helped her to put this new and satisfying relationship ahead of her constant worries about Jill because he could see Jill's growing independence more clearly than Leah could.

CHANGES IN CHILDREN'S BEHAVIOR

Some children become very sensitive to the relationship between their parents. They sense their parents' unspoken anger or tensions and can become quite expert at distracting the parents by acting out, getting in trouble, or needing special attention. For example, a child who has been aware during the day of her parents' unhappiness may wake up at night with nightmares and insist on climbing into bed with them. The parents then become concerned with the child's fears, focus on the child, and continue to avoid their own difficulties. The child's frequent visits to the parents' bed can also provide a good excuse for a poor sex life or a good subject for an argument the next morning.

After the parents are divorced, the same behavior may serve a new function. The child's getting into bed with her divorced mother can be comforting for both of them. The child's behavior can give the mother a reason to approach the father for extra help or continued involvement in the custodial minifamily. Child-centered problem solving can maintain a strong connection between the divorced parents.

When a New Person joins one of the minifamilies, some of these old patterns may change. The stepfather may oppose his wife's habit of letting the frightened child come to bed with her. He may suggest other ways of soothing the child's fears or resolving the underlying problem.

The following examples describe families in which changes set in motion by a New Person or a stepparent are beneficial to the parent and child.

FREQUENT ILLNESSES

Six-year-old Tina had always had frequent colds and ear infections, due to what the doctor thought might be an allergic condition. She tended to get ill when the unspoken conflict between her parents began escalating. Her illness would divert their attention from problems with each other and mobilize them around her care.

Effect on the Nuclear Family

Philip, Tina's father, was easily upset by his daughter's illnesses. His younger sister had died at age four. He remembered the pain and helplessness he had felt as a child. Tina's mother, Elizabeth, became very nurturant and babied her daughter when she was ill. Elizabeth would reassure Philip, and he would allow her to be close to him.

Parental Divorce

When Tina was six, her parents separated and intended to divorce. Tina visited her father regularly, often spending the weekend at his new apartment. She continued to become ill quite easily and had a series of strep infections the winter that her parents split up.

Her most common pattern was to start feeling sick on Saturday at her father's house. By late afternoon she might have developed a fever or become tearful about the pain in her throat. Philip would call his ex-wife frequently throughout the day to ask for advice or to have Tina talk with her. Elizabeth would not go out for more than several hours on a Saturday because Philip might call to say that Tina was feeling ill. Sometimes Philip would return Tina to her mother Saturday evening, feeling that he could not adequately care for her himself. Other times he would put Tina in the car, pick up Elizabeth, and drive the three of them to the doctor. Tina's illnesses were one way of making sure that Elizabeth was not too lonely on her weekends off.

New-Couple Relationship

Philip had been attracted to Anne before leaving Elizabeth, but he waited until he and his wife had been separated for several months before calling her. She was also divorced and she had two children. Their relationship developed rapidly.

One weekend Anne's children went to their grandparents' house, and she stayed at Philip's house. Saturday morning Tina was feverish and complained of a sore throat. Anne was used to sick children. After reminding Philip to set up the vaporizer for Tina and give her lots of juice, she went out for Popsicles and dot-to-dot books. When she came back, Philip called the doctor and arranged to take Tina in for a throat culture. Somehow, with Anne there, Philip didn't find it necessary to call Elizabeth. Philip and Anne took Tina to the doctor. Anne helped Philip put Tina to bed early, and the two adults had a late dinner by themselves. Tina tried to call her mother before going to bed, but Elizabeth, assuming that no news was good news, had gone to a movie.

Tina was nursed through several illnesses by Philip and Anne, or by Philip with Anne's help over the telephone. Anne calmed Philip's anxieties by giving him confidence in his fathering rather than by taking over Tina's care. Tina began to feel comfortable and secure with her father whether she was feeling well or ill.

Firmer Boundaries Between Ex-Spouses

With Anne's help, Philip saw that he could be a competent father. Philip's increased self-confidence enabled him to move further away from his ex-wife. The father-child minifamily became stronger. The ties between the mother, father, and child as one family were weakened, and Tina was no longer holding her parents' relationship together.

Mother's Reaction

Elizabeth felt excluded and upset the first few times that Philip brought Tina back ill on Sunday afternoon after not having called her about the illness. She was surprised when he left hastily and didn't give her a cough-by-cough account.

When she saw that he was not going to call her, however, she started using her child-free weekends to make new friends and do things for herself. She followed Philip's example and limited the number of times she called him about Tina.

New Couple

The new couple, Philip and Anne, gained more privacy when Philip and Elizabeth stopped talking to each other so frequently about Tina. If Anne came to Philip's house during the week, she could answer his phone without wondering whether Elizabeth would be on the other end. Philip no longer worried about Tina when she wasn't with him. He assumed that Elizabeth would provide the necessary care just as he did.

New Health

About two years after that first Saturday, when Anne helped Philip to make Tina more comfortable, Tina went through a whole school semester without any absences. Her pediatrician thought she had outgrown her propensity for strep infections and colds. Each of her parents had successfully made the transition from their marriage to a new life. Philip had married Anne, and her children lived with them. Elizabeth had moved into a large house with another divorced woman and was quite happy with her freedom.

Observations

Anne's role in boosting Philip's confidence was very important in the changes that took place. If she had rushed in to fill Elizabeth's position of providing direct care, Tina would have been resentful and might have found other ways of bringing her parents together. Fortunately, Anne's responsibilities to her own children prevented her from being totally available for this role.

Elizabeth was able to let go when she saw Philip becoming more independent of her. She realized that she could have a life of her own.

Tina's improved health might have been purely a result of physiological changes. However, she never developed other problems that would result in bringing her parents together.

ADOLESCENT ACTING OUT

Maxine's parents had been divorced for four years, since she was twelve. She lived with her mother, Adele, and had infrequent contact with her father, George. Her mother had been dating Walter for several years. He and Maxine had a friendly but distant relationship.

Announcement of Remarriage Plans

Adele and Walter told Maxine they were planning to marry; several days later she was caught shoplifting. Adele was extremely upset by Maxine's behavior. She was convinced it was a reaction to hearing about the remarriage. She decided to postpone the wedding date. As a result of shoplifting, Maxine was referred to a family counseling center.

Former Couple Communication

An immediate effect of Maxine's acting out was increased communication between her mother and father. They talked with each other about the plans for counseling and about being stricter with Maxine.

This was not the first time that mischievous behavior on Maxine's part had brought her parents into closer contact with each other. They were alarmed, though, that this time she had broken a law. Her behavior may have been a last-ditch effort to bring her parents back together before her mother's remarriage made a reconciliation impossible.

Counseling with Three Adults

The family counselor assigned to Maxine chose to include Walter in the counseling process. The counselor had several meetings at which Maxine, Adele, Walter, and George were all present. She also met with the new couple alone and with Adele and Maxine. Maxine was surprised that George, her father, was willing to include Walter in talks about a family problem and was even more surprised when the two men seemed to like each other. Her father's cooperation in the counseling seemed to be a seal of approval for her mother's new relationship.

Another Look at the Mother-Daughter Relationship

Maxine's past behavior had not only brought her parents closer together at certain times but had also moved them apart during either angry exchanges or intimate moments. For example, she had once broken a window while they were having an argument about money. When she was nine, she had prevented her parents from going on a "second honeymoon" by refusing to attend school for two weeks. Now that Adele was planning to remarry, Maxine was offering her mother a way out of becoming more committed, a good reason to postpone or cancel the wedding.

Adele came from a family in which women believed that intimacy could be dangerous. She had had an alliance with her own mother that had excluded her father. Maxine was expressing not only her own ambivalence about the remarriage but Adele's doubts as well. Adele had barely thought twice before postponing the wedding.

Maxine's role as a monitor of her mother's behavior had also kept her from having friends her own age. At sixteen she had never dated, been to a boy-girl party, or spent the night at a girlfriend's house.

The Stepfather's Position

Walter was the third child of a couple who were already in their forties when he was born. His older sisters were ten and twelve years older than he. They took a major role in his early care, but they left home when he was still a boy. He had become used to being lonely and feeling like an outsider in his own family.

As an adult, he had lived alone and never married. When he met Adele, he was in his late forties. He had to push himself to open up in this relationship, but he wanted to stop being a loner. Adele both needed him and allowed him to be independent. When she pulled away from him from time to time, or excluded him from her mother-daughter minifamily, he was able to wait until she was ready to move closer again.

When Adele postponed the wedding, Walter initially experienced a familiar feeling of disappointment. Once again he was being asked to remain an outsider. Then he did something very unusual for him—he became furious. The counselor had encouraged him to risk being angry. He acted on his own behalf, to take care of his own needs. He told Adele, with Maxine present, that married or not, he was planning to move into her house (according to their plan for after the wedding) on the original wedding date.

Adele, who had discussed her own fears about the remarriage in several individual counseling sessions, was ready to accept the challenge of more commitment and was genuinely excited by Walter's plans.

Maxine started to protest, but she was interrupted by Walter, asking her to help him find room in the house for his furniture and paintings. Otherwise, he said, the place will look like a furniture store. He told Maxine he thought she had good taste and would be very helpful. Walter's own anxiety about inclusion had made him sensitive to the feelings that Maxine might have in response to his plan. Adele suggested they visit Walter's apartment, which Maxine had never seen, to take a look at his "junk."

Walter made it clear that Maxine could not prevent his move, but he paid her a compliment and gave her a role in helping to bring together the parts of the new stepfamily. His request had several other functions. It demonstrated that he recognized something unique about Maxine, her good taste, and it put the process of his joining the mother-child minifamily into very concrete terms, moving furniture. Thinking about the practical aspects of the upcoming change reduced the anxiety for all three of them.

Adele was able to support Walter's demand for greater closeness even though she could not have initiated that change herself. By accepting Walter's plan, she expressed her loyalty to him, her greater independence from Maxine, and her own desire for the new relationship.

Shift in Power Between Mother and Daughter

Several weeks later Maxine was planning to go to her first slumber party. Adele and Walter had plans to spend the night at Walter's apartment and start packing his things.

That afternoon Maxine called the girl who was giving the party and said she could not come. Then she told her mother that she wasn't going. Adele phoned Walter to see if he thought they could spend the night at her house instead. He was angry that she wanted to change plans because of Maxine and threatened to stop seeing her if she did not show up at his apartment on time and alone.

Adele realized that she could not let Maxine come between her and Walter. She told Maxine that she could change her mind about the party or she could stay with her grandmother, and gave her one hour to decide.

Maxine cried and raged, but Adele remained firmer than she had in years. Maxine even called George, to see if he would intervene on her behalf, but he supported Adele's position. Finally, Adele dropped Maxine at her grandmother's on the way to Walter's.

Maxine may have opted out of the slumber party because it was a new social situation for her. Her mother's suggestion that she could stay at her grandmother's allowed Maxine to postpone becoming more involved with friends without continuing to control her mother's relationship.

By attempting one more time to keep her mother and Walter apart (remember they were planning to pack Walter's things), Maxine was trying to keep to the role she previously had with her mother. Adele, by honoring her commitment to Walter, resisted letting Maxine be in charge. When even her father refused to participate in Maxine's efforts to keep the door open for his return, her resources were exhausted.

The Visiting Minifamily

Although Maxine could usually bring her father into a crisis, her ongoing relationship with him was not close. She had been too attached to her mother to allow herself to be open to the visiting minifamily. Both while her parents were married and since their divorce, she had not felt that her father was worth knowing or that she had much to offer him. This is not surprising when we remember how ambivalent her mother and her mother's family were about men.

The counselor saw an opportunity to strengthen the visiting minifamily and give Adele and Walter more privacy to work on their relationship. She urged George to spend more time with Maxine and give her some special attention.

George began inviting Maxine to spend weekends at his house. Maxine agreed to the visits, though she felt uneasy about leaving her mother home alone with Walter. She actually enjoyed the time she spent with her father. Her relationship with him was less complicated than the one she had with her mother. He tried to find things for them to do together, and they shared making decisions and cooking. When Maxine grew old enough to get a driver's permit in her state, she asked her father to help her practice driving and take her for her test.

Although the changes in this family limited Maxine's power to bring her father into contact with her mother, they also gave her a direct relationship with her father. She learned to trust him even though he was a man and her mother had not trusted him. This helped her become independent from her mother and laid the groundwork for her to form adult relationships with men.

The Remarriage

Walter and Adele did get married. They spent several months in counseling as a couple to improve their communication and trust in each other. They realized they were both making important and positive changes in their personal development.

Maxine felt excluded from the new kind of intimacy Adele had with Walter. She learned, however, that she had a father on whom she could rely, and she began to make friends with her classmates. Adele and Walter, by regulating their own relationship, relieved her of a burdensome responsibility and established the expectation that she would control her impulses and behave in a socially acceptable manner.

AN OVERRESPONSIBLE CHILD

Lisa was eight when her parents separated. As the oldest child and the only girl, she quickly became her mother's assistant in caring for her brothers, who were four and three, and taking care of the house.

The Custodial Minifamily

In the eight years following the divorce, Lisa's mother, Louise, changed jobs seven times and lived in ten different apartments. Through all these changes, Lisa kept the three children functioning. She became the most stable member of the custodial minifamily.

Change of Custody

When Lisa was sixteen, her father, Nelson, and her stepmother, Debbie, became the children's custodial parents. They had requested a change of custody because Louise's unstable lifestyle did not seem good for the children. Louise initially refused but suddenly agreed.

Nelson had a very demanding job as a business consultant. Although he had been active in caring for the children on their weekend visits, he and Debbie agreed that Debbie, who worked only part-time and had a job close to home, would have to be the primary child-care person during the week. Consequently, Debbie had a more active role with the children than many other stepparents.

The children had come to accept Debbie as their part-time stepmother. They usually respected her authority and were friendly to her when they visited. Nonetheless, the change from a visiting stepfamily to a custodial stepfamily was not easy. The two boys, now twelve and eleven, resisted Debbie's attempts to care for them. They became withdrawn and shy with the children in their new school. They wanted to sit on Nelson's lap whenever he was home.

Lisa struggled with Debbie for the role of coparent to her brothers. Debbie wanted all the children to help around the house and the two adults to be in charge. Lisa was accustomed to taking over, doing chores her own way, and directing her brothers (they called it "bossing"). She would resist Debbie by not doing the chores assigned to her at family meetings and then cooking a surprise dinner when Debbie was at work.

Lisa's loyalty to her mother kept her from accepting Debbie's ways. Whenever Debbie told Lisa she was not responsible for her brothers, Lisa felt that Debbie was saying her own mother had been wrong.

New Bond Between Stepmother and Stepdaughter

Debbie had also had the responsibility of caring for her siblings, a younger brother and sister. Her mother had died when she was ten, and she had looked after her father's household. She had identified with Lisa ever since meeting Nelson. She felt sad when she saw Lisa missing her childhood just as she had.

One weekend the family went skiing. Debbie, an expert skier, taught Lisa the basics. Lisa caught on very quickly, and Debbie suggested that the two of them try some harder slopes while Nelson stayed with the boys. Lisa was surprised that she didn't have to stay with her brothers but could join Debbie. Her status as the oldest was now a privilege.

By a lucky coincidence, Lisa's high school was planning a ski trip for winter vacation. Lisa, excited about her skiing, was eager to go. The students were raising money to pay the expenses. The fund-raising activities took Lisa out of the house in the afternoons. For the first time in many years, she wasn't staying home after school watching her brothers, cooking dinner, or doing laundry. Debbie even volunteered to help Lisa make something for a bake sale. The ski trip plans introduced Lisa to a new group of friends. She began to enjoy herself.

Lisa began to appreciate Debbie and Debbie's way of dividing the chores so she was not overburdened. She began to obey the house rules and do the chores assigned to her. As Lisa became cheerful and cooperative, Debbie began to like her more and found time to spend with her on a one-to-one basis.

Mother as Visiting Parent

Lisa remained very loyal to Louise, who rarely visited the children and broke many of her promises to take them out. Lisa talked about going back to her mother's, as though her stay with her father was temporary. After living with their father for eight months, Lisa and her brothers went to stay with their mother for a ten-day school vacation, the longest visit they had had since the move.

Louise expected Lisa to take care of her brothers and the house as she had always done. Lisa could not say no to her mother or avoid fitting back into the familiar role of family caretaker, but she found herself missing Debbie. She called Debbie every night and told her she wanted to return to her father's home and stay there forever. Although she loved her mother, she wanted to be in a house where she had freedom to be a child in the family.

New Acceptance of the Stepfamily

After the long visit, all three children seemed relieved to be "home" with Nelson and Debbie. Lisa's open closeness with Debbie led the way for her brothers to see Debbie as a person who could nurture them. They began to feel safer in asking her for help. They began to share some of their feelings with her. Lisa was grateful for her freedom to be a teenager, and she appreciated Debbie's help in buying clothes and choosing courses at school. Debbie also listened to her concerns about friendships.

Debbie felt very proud of her role in providing a good home for her stepchildren. She was pleased to see Lisa having a happier adolescence than hers had been. Sometimes, however, she still felt more like Cinderella than the stepmother. She felt overwhelmed by the physical and emotional work of raising three children. She was angry at the children's mother for neglecting them and leaving her with the chores. She felt abandoned by the children when they ran off with their friends and left her with a mess to clean up. This new situation was so similar to the aftermath of her mother's death that she seemed to relive some of her childhood pain.

The Couple Relationship

Nelson also felt overwhelmed by the physical, financial, and emotional needs of his children. He would come home from work to two needy sons, a sullen daughter, and a wife who was both exhausted and exasperated. The weekends meant wondering whether Louise would show up for her visits, finishing a badly needed room in the attic, and listening to Debbie's complaints about the children.

It was only when the children finally went to Louise's for the long vacation that Nelson and Debbie realized how strained their relationship had become. They missed the things they had done together before the children lived with them. They agreed that their marriage might fall apart if they could not get more relief from the children's needs and find ways to give to each other and revive their intimacy.

Observations

Debbie could understand what Lisa needed because her childhood had been similar to Lisa's. She was able to structure a new stepfamily in which Lisa was freed from too much responsibility and too little support. However, she needed someone to rely on so that she would not overburden herself and do all the work without gratifying her own needs. She and Nelson would have to get together and find a way to nurture each other and their couple relationship.

SUMMING UP

The story of another stepfamily, told simply in a few pages, may seem to make more sense than your own family story. The patterns are clearer, and the choices stand out more. Your own life may seem more muddled and confusing.

Reading about other families can help you stand back and look at your own family's history for the last few years. How would you choose the turning points in your life? You may understand yourself better if you try to think about describing major events in your life to a stranger. Taking a perspective of years rather than months, months rather than weeks, and weeks rather than days is also helpful in seeing the changes in your stepfamily. Stepfamily development is a slow and complicated process.

In the stepfamilies in this chapter the minifamilies are intimately intertwined. For Philip, Gloria, and Janet, for example, there is not a clean break between the divorce and the remarriage. A new relationship is beginning as a marriage is ending. Even for Leah, who has been divorced a long time, echoes of the first marriage are evoked in her second marriage.

The minifamilies and stepfamilies cannot avoid influencing each other. A happy event for Dwayne and Elissa, their marriage, comes at a time when Leah and Bruce are mourning the death of his father. Dwayne and Elissa are not insensitive people; they would never have chosen to get married following a death in Leah's family, but they could not control the events that occurred. Anthony's efforts to help Teddy with his baseball made his stepfamily a closer one but interfered dramatically with Teddy's relationship with his father. Sometimes a change for the worse in one minifamily seems to improve life in another minifamily. Louise may have been devastated by the visit from her children during which Lisa realized she actually preferred living with her father and Debbie. Nonetheless, the visit resulted in a new closeness for the stepfamily of Nelson, Debbie, and the children.

There are also times when a change for the better in one part of the family is good for another part as well. Adele's plans to get married to Walter brought out, through a circuitous route, a chance for, her husband, George, to become closer to his daughter. These outcomes were positive for the adults and eventually positive for Maxine, but the day that Maxine was arrested would not have been considered a good one by any member of the family. Nonetheless, the counseling which resulted from the shoplifting helped them all. When you stand back far enough, many events in a family's history lose their definition as completely positive or negative.

The changes of the individual family members are also linked to the minifamily and stepfamily changes. Walter's desire to become more intimate was important to bringing about a fairly successful stepfamily. David's sense of rejection when his stepsons wanted to spend more time with their father was painful, but he learned to accept his own sensitivity to being excluded and to acknowledge the fact that Gloria really wanted him as a husband, not just as a stepfather for her sons.

Change takes place in many ways. A New Person or stepparent can begin a series of changes that has ramifications for every minifamily. Anne's ability to help Philip care for Tina changed the father-daughter minifamily, the ex-spouse minifamily, and the mother-daughter minifamily. David's financial contribution to Gloria's household began a series of changes in that divorced-remarried family. If you feel powerless as a stepparent, you may want to reread these stories to find the many ways, both dramatic and subtle, in which stepparents were strong agents of change.

In a stepfamily any one person or any one couple often has less control over the course of events than they would have in a nuclear family. Nonetheless, people in stepfamilies are not powerless. Although the children in these families had to make many adjustments to new living situations, they were by no means mere victims of the circumstances of their parents' lives. Glen and Stan, for example, made a big difference in their father's life and in the noncustodial minifamily. Jill was able to change her views about Elissa and to accept her father's remarriage. Even Maxine was finally able to act on her own behalf rather than protect her mother.

Sometimes outside events, such as Bruce's father's stroke or the ski trip planned at Lisa's school, have important effects on the stepfamily. Often changes occur unexpectedly. Pete started sending his checks on time after Gloria stopped worrying about them; Jill became fond of Elissa at a time when children are often the most resentful of stepparents. At other times, people act consciously and deliberately to mold their stepfamily lives. Gloria purposely let her children spend more time with their father when they wanted to. Debbie thought carefully about her role with her stepchildren. Adele, Walter, and George used counseling to help them plan and achieve the changes they desired.

Stepfamilies often discover resources they had ignored or underestimated. George did not know he had the capacity to be a better father, and Maxine did not know she had a father who could help her in so many ways. Debbie became an important helper and role model for Lisa, and Anthony was able to be a distant, but constant, stepfather for Teddy. If we had asked Adele several years earlier how she would respond if her only daughter had been arrested, she would probably have told us she would die. But she did not, and in the process of helping her daughter, she was able to find within herself the ability to develop a more satisfying intimate relationship with a man.

Every stepfamily is different. Opportunities for uniqueness abound because there are many family members, the histories they bring are complex, and the challenges to be met are great. The flexibility and imagination used by many stepfamilies to build a life that works for them is truly astounding.

Your family is probably not just like one of these six. You may, however, have recognized in their stories some turning points similar to your own, an echo of your own feelings, or some mistakes you have made or avoided. You may have compared yourself to them and felt you were further along or miles behind. Luckily, there is no race. If you are a stepparent, you may have been surprised and gratified to see the influence that stepparents do have in changing the stepfamilies they join. Their influence does not always occur in the ways they would most like. Yours probably does not either. Nonetheless, because families are systems, a new member cannot join one part of the system without having an effect on other parts as well.

If I could broadcast a radio message to the stepfamilies I have written about and those who are reading this book, these would be the five points I would most like all of you to remember:

1. Look how you've grown. Seriously. Take the time to stand back and look at your own family as though you were on the

outside. You may discover that you can now cope with situations that would have thrown you off balance several years ago. Maybe you can actually have a phone conversation with your husband's new wife or your ex-wife. Maybe you can miss a visit with your children and be gloomy for one hour instead of an entire weekend.

2. Be kind to yourself. Any one person is not responsible for the problems of the stepfamily. You may have made some mistakes; you may have had some hard times. Even if you have, you still have a chance to work things out better. You deserve your own respect. And while you're at it, you'll find it easier to be kind and respectful toward other family members as well.

3. Plan strategies for change and choose among the options you have—always with the understanding that you are not completely in control of the outcome. Although you cannot work miracles in your family, you can create a better home life by using the power you do have. Practice in forming and using strategies helps you to become effective and tactful.

4. Revise your expectations. Your stepfamily life is not apt to fit the image you had before you were married. Using the old standards and dreams as a measure is not fair to yourself or your current family members. This book may help you develop some new goals and new expectations for your stepfamily.

5. Remember your partner. Your relationship was the reason you created a stepfamily in the first place and brought your children into it. Nourishing your marriage will make the bad times easier and the good times better. Giving to each other enables you to give more love to yourselves and your children.

Notes

CHAPTER ONE

1. Paul C. Glick, "Remarriage: Some Recent Changes and Variations," *Journal of Family Issues*, vol. 1, no. 4, 1980, pp. 455–78.

2. H. Weingarten, "Remarriage and Well-being: National Survey Evidence of Social and Psychological Effects," *Journal of Family Issues*, vol. 1, no. 4, 1980, pp. 533–59.

3. Frank F. Furstenberg, Jr., and Graham B. Spanier, *Recycling the Family: Remarriage after Divorce*, Sage, Beverly Hills, CA, 1984.

4. *Ibid.*

5. U.S. Bureau of the Census, "Number, Timing, and Duration of Marriages and Divorces in the United States: June 1975," *Current Population Reports*, ser. P-20, no. 297, U.S. Government Printing Office, Washington, DC, 1976.

6. Robert S. Weiss also uses this term in his book *Going It Alone: The Family Life and Social Situation of the Single Parent*, Basic Books, New York, 1979.

CHAPTER TWO

1. Constance R. Ahrons and Morton S. Perlmutter, "The Relationship Between Former Spouses: A Fundamental Subsystem in the Remarriage Family," in James C. Hansen and Lillian Messinger (eds.), *Therapy with Remarriage Families*, Aspen System Corporation, Rockville, MD, 1982.

2. Harriet Whitman Lee, Family Law Counselor, 1854 Thousand Oaks Boulevard, Berkeley, CA 94707.

3. U.S. Bureau of the Census, *Statistical Abstracts of the U.S.: 1985*, (105th ed.), Washington, DC, 1984.

4. Andrew J. Cherlin, *Marriage, Divorce, Remarriage*, Harvard University Press, Cambridge, MA, 1981.

5. Frank F. Furstenberg, Jr., and Graham B. Spanier, op. cit.

CHAPTER THREE

1. U.S. Bureau of the Census, *Statistical Abstracts of the U.S.: 1985*, (105th ed.), Washington, DC, 1984.

2. E. M. Hetherington, M. Cox, and R. Cox, "Family Interaction and the Social, Emotional and Cognitive Development of Children Following Divorce," in V. C. Vaughan and T. B. Brazelton (eds.), *The Family: Setting Priorities*, Science and Medicine, New York, 1979.

CHAPTER SIX

1. Emily B. Visher and John S. Visher, "Stepfamilies in the 1980s," in James C. Hansen and Lillian Messinger (eds.), op. cit.

2. Lucille Duberman, *The Reconstituted Family: A Study of Remarried Couples and Their Children*, Nelson-Hall, Chicago, 1975.

CHAPTER EIGHT

1. Frank F. Furstenberg, Jr., and Graham B. Spanier, op. cit.

2. Andrew J. Cherlin, op. cit.

3. These figures are based on a study by Frank F. Furstenberg, Jr., at the University of Pennsylvania, reported in *Marriage and Divorce Today Newsletter*, vol. 8, no. 4, 1982.

4. *Ibid.*

5. These are figures from 1981 quoted in U.S. Bureau of the Census, *Statistical Abstracts of the U.S.: 1985*, (105th ed.), Washington, DC, 1984.

6. *The Random House College Dictionary*, rev. ed., Random House, New York, 1982.

Index